Tottering in My Garden

Tottering in My Garden

a gardener's memoir
with notes for the novice

Midge Ellis Keeble

CAMDEN HOUSE

For my children, Jon, Elizabeth and David,
and my grandchildren, Karina, Simon and Edward.

Camden House Publishing
Suite 100, 25 Sheppard Avenue West
North York, Ontario M2N 6S7

Camden House Publishing
Box 766
Buffalo, New York 14240-0766

Printed and distributed under exclusive licence from Telemedia Communications Inc. by
Firefly Books
250 Sparks Avenue
Willowdale, Ontario
Canada M2H 2S4

This edition published 1994
First printing 1994
Second printing 1995

Canadian Cataloguing in Publication Data

Keeble, Midge Ellis
   Tottering in my garden

Bibliography: p.
Includes index.
ISBN 0-921820-90-9

1. Gardening.   I. Title.

SB453.K43 1994   635   C94-930486-7

Published by Camden House Publishing
(a division of Telemedia Communications Inc.)

Firefly Books (U.S.) Inc.
P.O. Box 1338
Ellicott Station
Buffalo, New York 14205

Printed and bound in Canada by
D.W. Friesen & Sons
Altona, Manitoba

Cover illustration by Lisa Smith
Illustrations by Diana Thompson
Drawings by Angela Parsons
Photographs by John Bentham Photography and Gordon Keeble

Contents

Introduction

When I was asked how I learned to garden, by an earnest young woman who didn't know where to begin, I found that I didn't know where to begin either.

'It would take a book,' I told her.

This is the book.

There are purists who will say that it isn't a book about gardening at all, but I am prepared to put up an argument. If for you a garden is a picture of perfection in a glossy magazine, an exact science, a balancing of nitrogen, potash and potassium, or even a religion, we must part company right here. It can be a little of all these things, but research among my gardening friends and a long, hard look at my own experience of forty years in the fields and six gardens at my back have led me to believe that, in real life, it isn't all that straightforward.

The garden won't stand still long enough to be tied down to one picture or a single topic. It is possible to slap down a blueprint and send in the bulldozers, and it has been done, but few of us have the resources or the strength of character for this procedure, and many of us recoil from the cool, mathematical erasure of what was there.

There is always something there: the shape of the land, the natural growth, even the inheritance from a former owner. That isn't to say that it can't or shouldn't be changed. But the ordinary gardener rarely resorts to all-out combat; he inclines more to the guerilla tactics of skirmish, sortie and hasty retreat. I am one of the ordinary gardeners.

Left to our own resources we would do very well, but, as the work is done bit by bit and piece by piece, we become open to intervention and assistance of friends, family, hired helpers and books. Books! Magazines! Pamphlets! They give us ideas leading to delusions and disaster or to triumphs undreamed of, and how are we to know which it will be until we try it? Trial and error, time and weather lead to constant change in both the gardener and the garden. You can't pin it down. It won't stand still.

Perfection? A little perfection some of the time is what we settle for and, for most of us, this spells content.

I am not saying that this is as it should be. I am simply stating that this is the way it is, that this is what every young gardener should know: that gardening is an adventure, liberally laced with misadventure.

It is neither a ladylike nor a leisurely pursuit. The day of the trowel and that elegant basket, the trug, lies far in the past with the head gardener and his minions or, one hopes, far in the future when all will be serene in your garden. Then you can potter about cutting the long-stemmed flowers and tweaking off the occasional leaf.

In the meantime it's totter all the way. For years you will be held in thrall, as I was, by a long-handled shovel—to be precise, a round-mouth, hollow-back shovel. You will be bewildered by more strange characters and acquire more curious facts than Alice in Wonderland. Through your gate will come the neighbour's dog, cats, people, cows, front-end loaders and backhoes. Their paths, opinions and personal obsessions will shape the garden while you fight a vigorous rear-guard action. But there will be heady moments when you think you are in control. The regal lily will bend its head under the arm of the crabapple tree, the perfect rose will display its elegance against the hedge of yew, and you will know that you did that.

But back to the real world. You will have to deal with the house. There are few gardens where there isn't a house somewhere in the middle, and houses have far too much to say for themselves. They decide where the shade will fall, where there is a warm wall, and how tall the trees should grow. They hold up proceedings with their constant demands and then turn around and say you can't plant the begonias there.

And so I have included them all: the houses, the animals, the people. They are as real as the weeds. The gardener has to deal with them all for the simple reason that they are a part of the world where a garden grows and a part of the problem.

The problem, however, is human-size. At a time when we are weighed down with problems insoluble, when the face on television begins to look like our own, here is a place where, with a little wit, ingenuity and persistence, the answers can be found; life can resume its proper size and we can find ourselves again.

And, lastly, we should know that there will be time for other things. A garden is not the main theme of life. It weaves in and out, waits, disappears and reappears, providing a counterpoint to family, home and friends, giving colour and balance to life, challenges unending, and often a dash of the comic.

All this we can learn for ourselves. The time will come when a colour, a shape or a shadow will persuade us out the door, and then, if we look, touch, listen, the garden itself will become our own best teacher.

Note

The Notes for the Novice, which contain bare-bones information, could also prove useful for the experienced gardener: they can be handed over to those enthusiastic weekend guests who would love to help in the garden if they just knew how. (I recommend particularly dead-heading and the use of the shovel.) Armchair gardeners, after leisurely perusal, can settle back happily into their confirmed opinion that such activities are best left to the Parks Department.

I

Beginner's Luck

"Experience teaches"
— TACITUS

The First Garden

The great gardens of the world were the result of conscious intent on the part of both owner and architect. There are also gardens of less grandeur where the owner has known what he was about before he started. But in most instances, the average householder, particularly in North America, decides to have a garden because he has a yard. He has a yard because he has a house. And he has a house because he got married and then had children and they needed more room, so he bought a house with a yard. Now he has to do something about the yard.

When our first two children were very much present and a third was about to arrive, Gordon and I chose a small house in a small town north of Toronto. The inevitable yard, securely fenced, was intended to be no more than an out-sized playpen. The builder had tossed grass seed around and about, front and back, and this had grown thick and green, which should have told us something if we had known anything at all. But neither of us had planted a seed in our lives. We bought a fourteen-dollar lawnmower at Eaton's and Gordon cut the grass.

The playpen remained a playpen for about two years and then Jon was six, in first grade, and not to be hemmed in. Elizabeth shinnied up the fence and then up the nearest tree. David, a logical type, found something to stand on, unlocked the gate and walked out.

The yard was empty.

The day stays vividly in my mind. It was April so it could have been raining, but it wasn't. It was Monday so my neighbour Alice could have been washing her husband's socks, but she was out enjoying the sunshine. *House Beautiful* could have minded its own affairs and stuck to house interiors. I don't know who was responsible for the shovel.

It's all too late now and I can't turn back the clock. The day was bright with a warm sun. *House Beautiful* arrived and for reasons best known to itself had taken a flyer in the direction of gardening. It was a one-page article explaining how 'You Can Grow Enough Food for Four' in a fifteen-by-twenty-foot plot. The full-page colour picture showed lush green pea pods hanging from a neat trellis, chunky lettuces all in a row, tomato plants heavy with fruit, and beside all this a charming young woman, straight from the model agency, not a hair out of place, lightly holding a rake and smiling.

Magazine in hand, I strolled out into the sunshine. Alice was out in her yard, and leaning casually against the fence was a shovel. Alice said she didn't own it. I didn't own it either, but I picked it up and pointed it at the ground, and it slid down into deep, dark, moist, rich earth that turned over easy as breathing. Peering into the hole, I could see more of the same below. Alice came over to see what I was doing and picked up the magazine. Look at all that food! Think of the money we'd save! We read the directions carefully together and decided we had better follow them word for word. We were advised that, to grow this amount of produce in so small a space, it would be necessary to thoroughly enrich the soil.

We were standing on the site of an old cow barn and about three feet of pure compost, but to us it was only dirt and you grew things in it. So we enriched it. We turned over two fifteen-by-twenty-foot plots. It was a breeze. We added cow manure, bone meal, blood meal, wood ashes and then topped it all off with a load of topsoil. Between us, we must have spent a month's grocery money on rakes, hoes, weeders and seeds. Still following directions, we planted the seeds closely. The result was staggering.

My two-year-old, intrigued with all the activity, collected all the leftover seeds, stirred them vigorously in a cup, spread them over a square yard by the back door and jumped up and down on them. This was the first example of high, wide, intensive planting I had ever seen and was so successful I really should have paid more attention.

All three of us were now inundated with peas, carrots, beans, beets and tomatoes. In this small country town, every family had a garden, and immediate neighbours were delighted to hand over their surplus produce to us. Now they politely turned the other way, hoping we would not try to unload our bounty on them. What to do with it? We had no freezers and the only things we knew how to put up safely were the tomatoes. Gradually our basements were chock full of crimson jars; and the window-sills, inside and out, were lined with large, green globes turning relentlessly red. I knew Alice had come to the end of the line when I came out one morning to find her throwing rocks at her garden and yelling 'Stop!'

And though we laughed, it wasn't entirely a joke. We were both weary of spending what should have been the long, lazy days of summer boiling up still more jars of tomato chutney, which would never be eaten. That evening her husband quietly turned the vegetable garden under and put down grass. He had had it with beans, he said, and Alice was happily broiling a steak.

My husband too had gone shopping, but not for a steak. He had bought me a present, the best book on gardening he could find, a gold medal in honour of my green thumb. In my opinion, there's no such thing as a green thumb. Either you know what you're doing or you don't. As innocent as two Eves, Alice and I had been working in a gardener's paradise. Apart from the deep compost, we were on top of a hill with superlative drainage, in full sun and facing south. The weather had alternated between misty rains and sunny days—a fool's paradise where one could do no wrong. Alice was no fool. She had taken to sitting in a lawn chair and watching proceedings from there.

For me, there was no escape. The book of knowledge had arrived and the least I could do was glance through it. This was *The Complete Book of Garden Magic* by Roy E. Biles, published in Chicago by the J.G. Ferguson Publishing Co. It is now out of print, but it would be worth your while to search through second-hand book stores or your public library. I can't think of a more basic, encyclopaedic mine of information for the beginner.

The magic in which Mr. Biles believes is digging, sometimes

double digging. He is the advocate of the deep, wide hole; and in case you should feel tempted to modify a little, he tells you exactly how deep and how wide in feet and inches. If there is something you don't know, he soon makes sure that you do know. Innocence is destroyed.

Dipping gingerly into the pages, I found a chapter on bugs. Bugs? What bugs? Skipping that, I found a picture of hybrid tea roses. On page 123 there was a cross-section drawing of how to prepare a rose bed. Instruction: excavate the entire bed to a depth of two feet. I shall pause here to allow time for reeling around and protesting.

Roses, when clad in crimson velvet or ivory satin, reclining in the emerald green, are the first ladies of the garden. But they must have the best. Anything less and they look as though they should be hustled out of sight. You want either beautiful roses or no roses at all, so get hold of yourself.

Excavate the entire bed to a depth of two feet. Place five inches of gravel in the bottom and level off. That's for drainage. Now, so that earth won't filter in and destroy the drainage, cover the gravel with straw. Not leaves, they mat. No corn-stalks, they've been sprayed with atrazine. Clean straw, unsprayed. If you have leaves, chopped fine or rotted, you can mix them up with earth, wet peat moss and well-rotted cow manure, plus bone meal. About a foot of this rich mix goes in on top of the straw. Now fill to the top with good earth, enriched with more bone meal and compost if you have it. Bone meal won't burn plant roots, and roses adore compost. If you're buying topsoil, make sure it didn't come out of a cornfield and that it hasn't been loaded with chemical fertilizers.

You may now retire for a shower and a drink and let the bed settle. A good watering will help it firm down.

The general principle of preparing the bed before plants arrive is one worth following. Just as guests appreciate the effort you make to prepare for them, so do plants settle in more readily if the bed is ready and a good meal waiting. Easier for them and easier for you.

When the roses arrive, unpack and puddle the roots. (You have mixed earth and water in a pail to a thin soup and the roots are swished gently in this until the hair roots are coated; that is, if the nursery has not pruned all their hair roots off.)

Planting involves digging most of the topsoil out again. If you can find a straight piece of two-by-four, mark it with the spacing you have chosen and place it across the bed with the ends on firm, undisturbed ground. Hybrid teas are planted three feet apart to discourage black spot. Dig a hole at each mark, wide and deep enough for the roots to spread. Fill with water and let it settle. If it doesn't, this is no place for a rose bed. And be sure you have chosen a site facing south, protected from strong winds but allowing good movement of air. I wish you good luck on that one.

Now you need two people. While one person holds the plant against the board, so that you can see the graft will end up two inches below the top surface of the bed, the other sprinkles in topsoil until half the root is covered. Then punch it firm with the fist. (No air pockets, please.) Fill the hole to the top surface and stamp firmly with the feet. The usual time for this planting is in the spring when it would be wise to pile earth up gently eight to ten inches around the canes and leave it in place for two weeks. This prevents the new buds from drying out. The same process (earthing up) is followed with a fall planting, but then the soil is rammed in firmly, and remains in place until the following spring. When you carefully remove this extra earth, you should find fat little buds ready to leaf out. Where the grafts have settled to by this time is anyone's guess, but you've done your best. And I can assure you that *you* will have done it. Because no one else will.

In that first garden I built the rose bed just that way while Alice smiled from her lawn chair and passersby paused to enquire if I was putting in a new sewer connection. In time, they paused to enquire where on earth I had found roses like that, refusing to believe they were the same varieties they had themselves.

Much of the credit would have to go to the nursery that provided the plants, and blessed be they in memory. Buy only the best, if you can find the best. Each rose had a wide twelve- or fourteen-inch beard of hair-roots. These days, try as I will, I find nothing but violently pruned and waxed bushes, each with a short, three-pronged, hairless root. A rose this size must have had a root to start with, so why cut it off? Why do nurseries do that? If this enrages you as it does me, we could start a protest group. Roots for roses! Root for roots!

Years later, I purchased a large plant from a farmer who lived in this same district, and asked him how I should care for it. He gave me a long look and said, 'Joost poot 'em inna ground.' This was all the gardening lore needed in the first garden. The roses would have fared almost as well if I had joost poot 'em inna ground. In fact, this method was used for some specially ordered petunias. Each was in its own pot and packed like rare procelain. They were popped in with no preparation and won a prize in the local flower show.

This sort of procedure teaches you nothing, because we learn from our mistakes and from solving problems. There, I couldn't make a mistake even when I tried. A case in point was the King Alfred daffodils. These I had saved until my mother's arrival in November. I felt I should have the advantage of her expertise when planting.

'But your father did all that,' said Mama. Of course! Mother just cut and arranged the sweet peas and roses. The thought of her with a shovel in hand was not to be thought of, if that makes sense. She was the original gal with the trowel and the trug, but she felt I lived a hard life, so followed me out conscience-stricken, wrapped warmly in her tweed coat.

I arranged my tools and bags of bulbs and went to work. After a while she said, 'I am trying to remember, but I don't think Dad used a hammer and a chisel to plant bulbs.'

'But the ground is frozen. It's frozen hard.'

'I think they go in the other way up.'

'What?'

'I'm almost positive. They go in with the point up. The wide part at the bottom has all those little things on it, probably roots.' The chisel had made cone-shaped holes and the bulbs fit better point down, but I could see the sense of what she said, took all the bulbs out, re-shaped the holes and packed all the bulbs in with a plenitude of little cubes of frozen earth and air pockets.

'Well, I don't know,' said Mama and led me in for a cup of hot tea.

Perhaps the rains that followed did my planting for me, perhaps they would have come up even planted upside down. King Alfreds can take it. Nonetheless, I did not deserve the magnificent display they made the following spring.

I managed to make one mistake with this garden. I let it persuade me that I was a gardener.

On the other hand, every garden teaches you something. Though the flowers and vegetables have faded from memory, I remember that earth. I can feel it warm and rich in my hands like soft bread crumbs. It was dark, deep brown, not black, and it smelled good. Over the years I have kept trying to find it again.

NOTES FOR THE NOVICE

The Shovel and the Spade

The shovel has a round cutting edge with point. The spade has a straight-cut edge. The handle must be the correct length for your height. Use thereof:

1. Do not scoop. Scooping is for loading a barrow or scraping snow off the walk.
2. Point the shovel straight down to the south pole.
3. Keeping your back straight, simply stand on the shoulder of the blade and allow your body weight to send it down into the earth.
4. Step back to the ground and, using both hands, press down on the handle as with a pump.
5. Continue to cut down with the blade and press back on the handle until you have outlined the hole or trench you are digging.
6. Repeat this go-around if the earth is heavy, sending the blade deeper and pumping the handle harder.

For all garden work, train yourself to keep your back straight and use your weight and thigh muscles rather than the back.

The Hole

Once you have outlined the hole, remove the loose earth to a barrow. If it is poor soil, layer it in the compost heap. Back-fill the hole with good soil, to which you can add bone meal and/or rotted manure, using the barrow as a mixing bowl.

When the hole, straight-sided, is about 4 inches (10 cm) deeper and wider than the plant, return 2 or 3 inches (5–8 cm) of the mixed soil to cushion the bottom of the hole. Add 2 inches

(5 cm) of unmixed soil as a buffer between plant roots and fertilizer.

Half-fill the hole with water. If it doesn't drain away, dig a new hole. You *can* dig the hole deeper and add 4 to 6 inches (10–15 cm) of gravel or small stones. However, if the entire garden has poor drainage, see the next chapter, The Clay Garden.

The Plant

POTTED: Slit the sides of the pot from top to bottom in four or five places. Bend the flaps down to the ground so that the plant can be lifted or slid into the hole.

BURLAPPED: Untie and loosen from stem. Check to see that there is no rope or string burn around stem. If bad, return to grower. If slight, seal with tree paint. Burlap left under the plant in the hole will rot, but I prefer to lift or slide plant into hole without.

TRANSPLANTING: When the new planting hole is prepared and half-filled with water, use the same procedure for removing the plant as you used for digging the hole. Cut straight down well out from the plant so that you don't cut roots. On the second go-around, jiggle the handle to tease the fine hair roots loose from the soil without breaking. When the entire plant is loose and rocking in the hole, remove quickly to its new home. Fill around the plant with good topsoil within 2 to 3 inches (5–7 cm) from the top. Water down to remove air and add more dry soil. Now punch down with fists or, for large plants, tread around lightly with feet. Leave a slight depression to catch rain.

Use the above technique for the transplanting of everything from small plants to trees. N.B. Here is your one opportunity to place food and water below the root area—don't miss it. Moved in this manner, your plant will suffer nothing more than a little mild astonishment.

The Transplanting of Small Annuals

The bed should be prepared and worked to a fine tilth. Break up to a dozen plants apart from the flat and place exactly where you want them, adjusting the spacing. With your trowel, scoop out a hole and pop in the plant. Using a watering-can, fill each hole with water around the plant root. Now go back and, with your two hands, scoop earth and press down to anchor your plants. This system (ten to twelve at a time) is fast and spaces properly. With water below, the leaves will stay crisp as cos lettuce. (No: watering from above does not work as well.)

The Clay Garden

We left Eden for the real world. It's stretching things a little to regard Don Mills as the real world, but in our search for good schools and civilization we had come on developments mired in mud, enveloped in dust, without roads and all waiting for better times. So when we found Don Mills, a suburb north of Toronto, with its roads in place and grass back and front, it seemed by comparison to be civilization.

It was September when I ventured out into the yard to find that the grass had been ironed out on all the packed-down rubble of building. Bulldozers had smashed down every tree and the sun had blazed down all summer, burning everything to a crisp. The real world was literally a hard place.

If I had come to this garden first, I would not have been labouring under the delusion that I had a green thumb; I might never have gardened at all. But someone had tucked that shovel into the moving van. When I took it outside, it slithered along the surface of the ground, utterly useless.

There was a very industrious gardener on the thirty feet to the west of us. He was out edging the edges of what we all laughingly called the lawn. He was importing topsoil by the truckload and dumping it down wherever he wanted a flower bed, but if a shovel wouldn't penetrate what lay underneath, neither would water. Wishing him well, I retired to the house in search of Roy E. Biles and *Garden Magic*.

Mr. Biles said, 'Dig a trench four feet deep.'

I came out of shock late the following afternoon and reached for the phone. My good friend Rox had just completed a small garden in Toronto clay. She was sure to have the answer. She had.

'Well, dear, yes. Clay is a problem. You break it up with a pick, adding fresh, hot horse manure and sand. Now, even though my garden is postage-stamp size, there was no way I could do all that, so I laid brick in lieu of grass,' she said. For flower beds she had edged with railway ties, broken the clay underneath, adding the aforesaid sand and manure, and filled up with topsoil. These drained reasonably well.

'Of course, as you know, there is no access to my yard except through the front door,' and she went on to describe the horrors of wheelbarrowing bricks, gravel, manure and topsoil through the front door, down the hall and out the back.

A stimulant was needed. I brewed coffee and returned to Mr. Biles. I had realized, and Rox had made it clear, that the problem was drainage, the same problem you can have with a plant with its roots in standing water. It will drown. What I had was a fifty-by-thirty-foot flower pot, filled to the brim with fine grey clay.

If you can percolate the fine particles out of clay you will be left with friable soil. At the same time, you will lower the water table so that the roots of trees, shrubs and flowers will reach down deep to find the water and so survive through the dry days of summer. How do you percolate the fine particles out of clay?

You dig a trench four feet deep.

The trench starts at four feet, sloping down one foot for every hundred feet, leading to a dry well or hole six feet deep. The dry well is filled with cinders or gravel. Once the trench is dug it is lined with gravel, preserving the slope, and on this you lay farmer's tile—an eight-inch tube of red clay (the same weeping tile the builder placed around the foundation of your house). The tiles are placed an eighth of an inch apart and secured with earth to keep them in line when you back-fill. Back-fill with good topsoil to start, a few inches. If you have to go round a corner, cover the joint with tarpaper and cement—because you don't want to trap water, do you? Now you replace all that mountain of earth at the top of the trench. Such a trench will percolate the soil fifty feet on either side. The same technique will drain a field of standing water. Farmers call it 'tiling'.

A little work with a tape measure told me that what we

needed was a trench four feet deep and eighty feet long, down the side of the yard and across the back. And a six-foot hole. And someone to dig it.

I paid a few informal calls on the construction crews still working in the district and learned that there was no help there. Dig a ditch? Indignation on all sides. So I ran an ad in the paper. In a city of two million people, only one replied. I told him I wanted a man or men to dig a four-foot trench eighty feet long and waited to hear the click of the receiver.

'Yes?' he said.

I said they would need picks as well as shovels.

'Right.'

Recklessly I added the six-foot hole.

'When d'you want it? Tomorrow?'

'Tomorrow would be fine,' I whispered and gave him the address.

The two young men who arrived the next day have been a mystery to me ever since. They had shoulders like wrestlers and fine teeth flashing in wide grins. Armed with picks and shovels, they went straight to work, laughing as if it were all a great joke and never pausing to ask what I thought I was doing or what it was all for. Gordon had persuaded me to modify the plan a little and start at three feet, sloping to four. When all I could see was their heads, I went out to say, 'Aren't you too deep?' They handed me a tape measure and pointed out that they were both a little short in the leg.

Broken bricks, tin cans and a long white bone appeared. The bone, they assured me, was the thigh bone of a deer. 'You never know what you'll find down here.' This is all too true, as the telephone, hydro and gas companies will tell you. Before you dig trenches, find out just what *is* down there.

Eventually the boys disappeared altogether in the six-foot hole. They were still all smiles and gaily waving as they drove off in their half-ton truck, and I hadn't thought to get their names or phone number. Were they in from the farm or travelling across the country doing odd jobs? I'll never know, and oh! how I've needed them since. Once you find your true love or a man who will dig, never let him go!

Laying the tile on the gravel was simple, but all that mountain of earth had to go back in. That would have been simple, too, if it hadn't rained. The ditch filled with water and the earth grew sodden and heavy. Jon pointed out that, if I waited for better weather, it would set like concrete. Pulling on his rubber boots, he led me out to help him shovel, push and heave. We finished in the dark, the pouring rain and deep silence.

The interest of our neighbours had reached fever pitch. 'How long before it works?' The real question was, 'Will it work?' Conversations took place over the garden fence on all three sides, and the following year all agreed that the grass was definitely greener on our side of the fence. In time, there was bounce to the turf.

What is obvious to me now, and must have been to you all along, is that there was no need for all that hand-digging. A backhoe or trencher, with a good operator who will grade carefully, is all that is needed, plus checking first for gas mains, power lines and whatnot. In fact, if you are building a house on clay soil, the man who puts in your weeping tile can do the whole job. The advantage is that it works forever and can improve the soil in the whole garden. Once plantings are in, you can't very well work with a pick or fresh manure, a method I tried later and found only temporary. Mr. Biles was right again. If you wish to defeat clay, once and for all, dig a trench four feet deep.

Gordon and Jon were less enthusiastic, and Mr. Biles had disappeared. He was found, months later, at the bottom of a carton, deep in the darkest corner of the basement, where they had hidden him. Their defence was that the man never wanted a hole less than two feet deep. In an attempt to lead my thoughts away from holes, trenches and ditches, they produced another book. This was Helen Van Pelt Wilson's *Perennials Preferred*. 'Look at all the pretty flowers,' they said. One glance and I had to have them all.

Both *Perennials Preferred* and *Helen Van Pelt Wilson's Own Garden and Landscape Book* are now out of print; they were published by Doubleday. How to retrieve them for us all? They are still my favourite reading on a dull winter's day, and they are not coffee-table books, but are as workmanlike and informative as the more technical *Garden Magic*. The beds should be thoroughly prepared and the holes dug, wide and deep, the lady says, but these dull details are left behind as she weaves drifts of colour in her borders, plants ferns and Virginia bluebells beside her brook, or prunes to reveal the bare bones of a tree.

I didn't have a brook or a tree, but I had to have those flowers, all of them, no matter how Mrs. Wilson warned against the jumble that can ensue.

A perennial or herbaceous border should be wide and deep if it's to look like anything at all, and it should be planned on graph paper. Since the shovel would now go happily into the ground, I could manage the wide and deep, going thirty feet across the back and coming forward twelve feet. This was small, but it was all the space I had. The soil needed help, so all the good stuff—bone meal, rotted manure, humus—was worked in. Then I ran into a problem. I couldn't get it down on paper. If you are clever with graphs and crayons and can visualize your border at eye level by making a plan with a bird's-eye view, it is definitely the way to go. I remember feeling quite guilty, going my own way, simply ordering the shrubs and plants I liked and standing them about on the earth until an appealing pattern appeared.

In some ways it worked; in others it didn't. For instance, a plant labelled eighteen inches may decide to shoot up to three feet. You can move it. Then, nurseries love to substitute a bright orange lily for a pale yellow, or pink phlox for white, so you now have pink backed up with orange where you had planned white backed up with pale yellow. There isn't a piece of graph paper or a crayon that can save you from all that. Choose your nursery with care and mark your order NO SUBSTITUTIONS. Better still, mark your order *ABSOLUTELY NO SUBSTITUTIONS*. And know that where the catalogues say pink they mean purplish, coral means red, blue means purple, true pink means peach. The colour photographs aren't true, and you have no way of knowing the real colour until the plant is in flower.

Borders look best with a background of dark green trees or old, high brick walls, more easily found in England than in North America. As all I had was a low wire fence, this was screened with flowering crabapples of varying heights. Delphiniums, tall asters, and a few tall lilies came next behind drifts of phlox. Groups of peonies anchored down and broke up the lines of phlox and the whole was faced down with what few low-growing perennials I knew. Petunias took the place of the tulips as they died down. My drifts were more like rows, I had everything in there I could think of, and the colour scheme was not all that it should have been, but it was a marvellous introduction for a beginner. At last, I was making the acquaintance of a real variety of useful and attractive plants.

It's like being sent to a new school or thrust into the centre of a cocktail party where you know absolutely no one. Courage! Step right in there and you'll find someone you like; you may even make a lifelong friend. Beds of petunias or marigolds are all very nice, but they will teach you little or nothing. Try a perennial border and remember: deep and wide, pack it full, really swing your drifts, and let some of the tall boys step forward. You'll have a wonderful time.

The neighbours admired my herbaceous jumble and assured me I had a green thumb. Hah! Now I knew better.

NOTES FOR THE NOVICE

Perennials for All Seasons

AQUILEGIA (Columbine)

Grow your own from seeds: the hybrid McKana's Giants are my preference. Tuck them here and there in the garden where their airy blooms will lighten the look of the more stolid plants. Seeds will give you all the pastels, including a pure yellow if you are lucky. Dust with rotenone before blooming (as soon as the leaves are young and green) to defeat the infinitesimal caterpillar that will eat every leaf if you let it. Rotenone will control leaf miner as well.

My columbines do well in sandy soil, sun or shade, and last well into the peony season if well watered. Cut the stems well down into the bush, leaf stems as well, as they fade and new bloom will appear intermittently. I sow a new crop every three years and don't bother with dividing. Many sow themselves.

CAMPANULA (Harebells, Bellflowers)

Campanulas include many species. I list only two dependables here.

The Blue Clips Carpathian harebells (*C. carpatica*), about 6 inches (15 cm) high, bloom at the front of the border from June to September. (I do clip off the seed heads from time to time.) Grown from seed years ago, they continue to thrive and spread just enough to allow the lifting of a clump to fill an empty space. Very satisfactory.

My peachleaf bellflowers (*C. persificolia*) were purchased plants. They grow to 18 inches (45 cm), taller when in the mood, and are so delicate and entrancing with their white bells in late June that I put up with their short-lived beauty, preserving it with finicky clipping for as long as possible.

CHRYSANTHEMUM (including Shasta Daisies)

The season here is too short for the chrysanthemums I grew from seed. Buds would freeze before they had a chance to open. Now I purchase started plants in bloom, which, though expensive, have the advantage of showing their colours before I plunge. I favour Grenadine for the side garden because its rust-rose is happy with the rosy red brick and lives kindly with the last of the climbing roses. The yellows, bronzes and deep reds will invite the colours of the turning leaves into your garden and help to cheer you all the way into November.

My shasta daisies (*C. leucanthemum*) were grown from seed long ago and have been divided and given away by the bushel basket. They like the raised bed, the sandy loam and the sun. These are single and their crisp linen white is exactly what is needed for the hot days, but by August they are gone. I have now planted doubles, which I am told will last out the season. As the bloom dies, cut back the stem to a strong leaf so that you still have the green-leafed bush, which is bearable (but only bearable) in appearance.

DELPHINIUM

Grow the Pacific Giants from seed, or Blue Fountains if you want the blue without the height.

Delphiniums like a rich limey soil and a northern site, and they do need air circulation, being subject to mildew. Spray with Safer's Natural Fungicide when you spray your roses. Coal ashes are good around the shallow roots, but who has coal ashes? Use wood ash or sharp sand instead. Don't allow earth up over the crown at the base of the stems. After first bloom, cut the stem down low but leave old foliage to protect new growth until it is 8 inches (20 cm) high. In a long season you may get second bloom.

Feed in early spring and late fall with bone meal, sheep manure and wood ashes, which they like best of all.

I now have long, dark green metal stakes, but the wind still snaps down the heads of the very tallest plants. These I have tucked in between phlox, which support them. They do mildew at the base, but the heads are a lovely accent when near a lily. The books say to pinch each plant back to three or four strong stems, but I don't know anyone who does.

Delphiniums really are a problem but they really are worth all the fuss. You can try the annual larkspur if it grows tall enough to please you.

HEMEROCALLIS (Day Lilies)

These trouble-free lovelies can bring you through June and on into September if you choose earlies, middles and lates. They come tall and they come small. The hybridizers are producing new colours, but I cling to the clear yellow and gold, such as the old Hyperion with its singing yellow and a clear vein of green under the petal. The dwarfs, some in a dusty buff orange, grow 12 to 18 inches (30–45 cm) high at the front of the border.

Like wildflowers, day lilies will grow under a careless hand, but they show their appreciation if you feed them phosphate and potash and give them sun in a good soil. Give them space to begin with (they do spread) and you will still have to lift and divide. Keep their raggedy blooms picked off (neatness counts). When all the blooms of a stem are gone, cut the stem at the base and leave the fountain of narrow green leaves, which will still be attractive when they go to gold in the fall.

HEUCHERA (Coral Bells)

Years ago I grew three flats of these from seed and used them to edge all the beds of the side garden. I still think it the most satisfactory edging of all. The delicate rose to red bells rise on thin stems from a cushion of green leaves. When the flowers die off, pluck the stems out. A few will still bloom in August, but even without the flowers you will have an informal green edging all season long. They lift out with a woody root and replant to fill a space with no trouble.

IRIS

Iris are delightful in the perennial border, but I plant mine on a south slope where they can toast their toes in the sun. *NO MANURE!* They are happy in good soil, in sun, protected from the invasive grass they seem to attract. Weed delicately by hand so as not to damage roots. If the weeds get out of control, lift the irises, divide and plant in a new, clean bed.

They need dividing about every three years. After hosing them off, I cut mine apart in about three. This is the time to cut away soft or diseased parts from the rhizome and clip back the blade-like leaves to about 8 inches (20 cm), shorter on the sides and higher in the middle, in a fan shape. Now place the fleshy rhizomes, all in the same direction, a foot (30 cm) or more apart with the top barely beneath the soil and the hair roots fanned out. August is the time for this operation. Both spring and fall, pull away and destroy all old leaves. Feed as for peonies, especially bone meal, but less generously.

I stake the tall bearded iris at the base only with a small metal rod, easily hidden. The foliage turns brown in late August, so mine are planted behind a retaining wall, where leaves are hidden but the flowers soar well up into sight in June. Now there are beautiful pinks and peaches, as well as all shades of blue.

OENOTHERA *(Sundrops, Evening Primrose)*

My Ozark sundrop (*O. missouriensis*), a purchased plant, grows low to the ground, produces a large golden bell and has huge fascinating seed heads, which I hate to remove. The bloom picks up the yellows of the day lilies and of its cousin, evening primrose (*O. tetragona*).

PAEONIA *(Peonies)*

Plant singly as a base for a perennial border or a good 3 feet (1 m) apart when you want them for a hedge. Give them a rich, deep bed as for roses (p. 10), as they should stay in place for many years. They can live to be a hundred and handed on as heirlooms, so buy from a specialist and try to get six- to ten-eye roots. (Wild's of Missouri, my favourite supplier, will mail to Canada as well as throughout the U.S.)

There are hundreds of new varieties so that you can choose for colour, fragrance and time of blooming—early, mid-season and late—giving a sequence of bloom. Rich red (Red Charm) through rose (Doris Cooper, Jules Elie), the old white (Festiva Maxima) and the creamy singles (Carrara) are the reliables I cling to, though Festiva Maxima is felled every year by heavy rains. The singles come through the downpours smiling. I gave up on peony rings long ago and now use the strong four-ringed tomato cage, which is soon out of sight under the large green leaves.

Feed generously. I give them two good scoops of bone meal and the same measure of treated sheep manure spring and fall, plus manure tea when I am dispensing tea in mid-season (see p. 108).

When bloom is over, cut back the stem close to the ground and leave the glossy green bush as background to other flowers. It will turn a beautiful bronze in fall. Once limp with frost, cut it close to the ground and dispose of the foliage—away from the garden if botrytis blight is a hazard. Our winters go from 10°F above (-12°C) to 20°F below (-30°C), but, as we have snow cover, we don't mulch peonies; nor do they require spraying. You can ignore the ants unless they make ugly hills in the bed, in which case empty a pot of coffee on the hill and scatter the used grounds about. Works like magic.

PAPAVER (Oriental Poppies)

Buy the plants. They bloom early and briefly but hold the spot-light when they are on stage. Since the foliage is dreary, plant behind a rock, as I do, where the leaves can be folded down out of sight and left until new green growth appears in fall.

PHLOX

Purchase good cultivars or beg for contributions from your friends. The loveliest I have came from other gardens and generous friends. The pure whites, which I purchased, have a large heavy bloom; varieties of the pale pink or white with the red eye and a deep carmine have far more grace, and last and last through rain, wind and sun. Plant in drifts or in a bed of their own. Give them deep watering and a 2-foot (60-cm) bed of good soil, but keep the leaves dry to avoid mildew. Safer's Natural Fungicide and air circulation are your best defence.

There are two schools of thought on persuading the bloom to last. Some growers just shake the heads to remove the seeds and tiny petals, but others clip just below the full flower-head. Then the side shoots should provide new bloom, rather in the fashion of broccoli.

September is the time to divide (about every three years), discarding the worn-out centre and replanting healthy clumps of five to six stems. This is when I cut the plant back to 6 or 8 inches (15-20 cm) in order to see where they are, come spring.

Clean out the tiny phlox leaves popping up in the bed, as these won't grow true to colour.

PLATYCODON (Balloon Flower)

If you love blue in the garden, *P. grandiflorus apoyama* is for you (the white and the rose are equally lovely). Eighteen inches (45 cm) is the correct height, though I have one that, for reasons of its own, grows as high as the day lily behind it. Before the flower opens into a star-shaped bell, the bud holds in the shape of an aerial balloon, which will delight visiting small children. I couldn't be without it.

This is merely a list of the old reliables. As you gain in experience, curiosity and courage, you will want to try the new and unusual. For a tempting smorgasbord of perennials, have a look at *Perennials: How to Select, Grow & Enjoy*, by Pamela Harper and Frederick McGourty. Pore over the catalogues and take your camera to other gardens, especially botanical gardens. You are sure to find something to astound the neighbours.

The Sand Garden

When your children know what they want, where it's at and how to get it, there's little you can do but climb on the bandwagon. Our daughter, who had spent her early years hanging upside down from the trees, was now right side up and clinging to a *barre* at the National Ballet School. Her brothers, almost equally focussed on their goals, had chosen schools in the heart of Toronto. We, their parents, tagged along and bought a small house in Rosedale, which is almost in the heart of Toronto.

It was an Eliza Doolittle of a house with a pretty Georgian face but badly in need of a good bath, and that is literally what it got. This time, David put on the rubber boots and led me into the basement. Here we spent an afternoon hurling pails of hot soap suds at the ceilings, walls and floors. He then turned on the hose full force and sluiced down everything, including me, while I swept fifty years' accumulation of whatever down the basement drain. Once it was aired out and dry, a man came to paint it white. I asked him if he could paint the entire house, inside and out, in a week.

'If you keep it simple and I hire enough men, why not?' said he. While his men swarmed over the walls, a wrecking crew hurled the kitchen cupboards out the door and installed pre-builts. The floors were refinished and Eliza was almost a lady.

One thing remained to be done. We had removed an old crystal chandelier, which was hanging lop-sided from the hall ceiling, and an evening was spent with the whole family lovingly washing each crystal and carefully replacing all its little wires. The main electrical feed was turned off and the chandelier rewired to the ceiling while Jon manned the switches below, and we all stood by prepared to cheer.

'Throw the switch!' yelled Gordon. Jon did. And all the lights in the house blew out.

The whole house was rewired and, once the chandelier sparkled beside the staircase, everyone said, 'How charming.' Eliza really was a lady at last.

No one had had time to look at the garden. Even I had a career, and we shot off in all directions early in the morning, returning to bury our noses in books and papers at night. As I flew past the stingy little borders in the back, I could see that the plants were not quite dead. On the other hand, they were not quite alive. Clay again, I thought, but this time we would use a machine to dig that trench. The garage debouched on a back lane, where a very dead tree sat in a grass plot by the garage wall. Next came a post-and-wire fence held up only by its wire. It would be easy enough to knock the tree and the fence down and let in a backhoe. Meanwhile, the boys cut the grass and tossed the clippings over the fence. Winter came, the snow covered all, and my conscience had a rest.

But spring does come again. April brought a slower pace and the urge to walk about and see what little surprises the former owners had left us. How could a house be this old and no one have cared enough to put in anything but that sad shrub? How long since anyone had worked up the earth in the borders? A closer look revealed that it wasn't earth. Neither was it clay. It was sand. I don't mean that it was sandy soil; I mean coarse, grey, gritty sand.

Following the prescription in the books, we worked in bales of peat moss, great bags of treated manure and chemical fertilizers. All of this mysteriously disappeared. New plants managed to just hold on in the dry sand which let everything else slip through its fingers, including the rain.

For every problem there is always an answer, but sometimes you have to wait for it. I sat out in the weak spring sunshine, reading and waiting and waving lazily at the train-man. Once a day, a train tootled slowly by on the track that ran along the back of the lane. The engineer waved at everybody and we all waved back, very friendly and rather nice.

The answer came in May. One bright morning, as we all stepped out the back door, we were halted in mid-flight. What was that? A cloud of full and glorious white bloom had appeared behind the fence. Our totally dead tree was very much alive. We discovered its roots were snaking above ground, twisting in and out of a dark, crumbly substance . . . the rotted grass clippings.

Scrabbling with our fingers, we managed to fill only one bushel basket, the tree roots were so thick. But even that one bushel spread on the flower borders brought everything to life. The reason is, of course, very simple. Everything we had added up to then had been sterile. The grass clippings were very much alive with bacteria. Earthworms appeared from heaven knows where. We collected more clippings, added egg shells and rotted leaves, and topped the beds before this mix was quite ready, but the plants and the earthworms were hungry enough to take it, ready or not.

Compost. For me, compost will forever be the real garden magic. Live food for live plants, forever renewing the earth, improving its structure, correcting both acid and lime conditions, mulching out weeds—and it's free. I swore I would never be without it again, and I never have. Over the years, I have built compost heaps carelessly, carefully and by accident, and will talk about that later. The main thing to remember now is just to toss anything that was once alive into an out-of-the-way corner and let it rot. The only exceptions are meat and bones. Everything else goes in, though if you are nervous about odours, stick to grass clippings, egg shells, dead leaves and a sprinkle of earth. When I drive along city streets in the fall and see great trucks hauling away all the leaves I could weep, and so could your flowers and shrubs. Rake your leaves and clippings into a corner and toss a net over them if you don't want them blowing around. Box them or bag them—leaving holes to let the air in—but don't throw them away. They're pure gold.

Looking back, it seems as though the moment a garden had taught me whatever it had to teach, I was moved up to the next class and new problems. While we had been so busy refurbishing house and garden, the CNR, equally busy, had been building a new shunting yard. By midsummer it was ready, and the first our neighbourhood knew about it was when a seventy-five-car train, hitting fifty miles an hour, came thundering down the track past our back doors. Nobody waved. I dearly love trains. I think they're romantic, but that doesn't mean I want one in the garden. You can imagine my reaction when a gentleman handed his real-estate card in through the front door and said he had clients interested in buying our house.

I sat him down in the living-room and, as a train went by, shouted, 'They know about . . . ?' and waved a hand vaguely at the trembling walls.

'Oh, yes,' he roared back. 'Sensitive to noise, are you?'

'Sorry?'

'I can find you a quiet house. Quiet! For you!'

The train rumbled off into the distance and he said he would find us a quiet house if that was what we wanted. That was what we wanted.

The Shade Garden

The new old house was quiet. Correction: it was funereal. Our stay there was so brief it hardly deserves a paragraph. Large oak trees, awful in their solemnity, shaded the entire back garden. By now I had found my dear Mr. L. to help with the decorating. We chose a deep moss green for the rug and, though I had lost my heart to an Italian silk, rich, glossy and the colour of divinity frosting, he gently refused to let me have it: too expensive, and too much else to be done on a small budget. So the fabric was green, rich and glossy and a quarter of the price, allowing us to re-cover the sofa. In green—what else? All this was done on a sunny day, and we had both lost sight of what happened on a rainy day. It was still serene, relaxed and quiet, but had rather the effect of living under water or in a subterranean cavern—a green gloom.

The green gloom motif was picked up and repeated outdoors, accentuated by five magnificent oak trees in the back and a strong line of ancient maples at the front. Under the thick canopy of leaves, there was only lily of the valley, beautiful but brief in season. In one open corner lilac flourished, so we did our best here to loosen the soil with pick, sand and manure. Not madly successful. Oak leaves fall in a thick, dank, leathery mat, take forever to disintegrate and work better than black plastic for choking off all growth beneath. A landscape firm presented me with a neat little graph, showing lots of evergreens, to which I could only say, 'Sorry I bothered you.'

If we had stayed, serious thought would have had to be given to a shade garden. Recently I was asked to suggest a perennial that would flower from spring to fall in the shade. There is no such thing, unless you count hostas, which will supply large green leaves, patterned with white, and a white or pale blue flower, late in the season.

In the end I suggested that the young lady first modify the shade, which could mean the expense of felling one or two trees. All growing things need light to manufacture their food, but it need not come from full, open sun. Many plants are happier in indirect light or dappled shade and, rather than losing a tree, the gardener may prefer high pruning, that is, the removal of low-growing branches, leaving a tall straight trunk, and the thinning out of the top branches to allow light to filter through. Both felling and pruning of this kind are for professionals only: first, there is the danger to interested bystanders; next, to the neighbour's roof and to the operator himself. As well there is the risk to the tree, which should be entrusted only to the hands of a skilled man if it is to survive in beauty and splendour. He is best found through word of mouth rather than advertising.

Under oak trees the soil will be acid, that is, with a pH of less than 7.0 (normal). Simple testing kits are available for the home gardener at most nurseries. The addition of lime is sometimes advised to raise the pH, to make the soil more alkaline, but in this case I would stay with what I had, add treated fertilizer and humus for compacted soil, and plant the acid-lovers: azaleas and rhododendron. They will flower spring and fall.

With dappled shade and acid soil there is a wonderful opportunity to establish a planting of wildflowers (now available from many nurseries): hepatica, trillium, jack-in-the-pulpit, lots of ferns, bleeding heart and, where the bed drifts out into more light, an edging of primroses and violets. Add a few small bulbs and you have a delightful picture for spring.

Choose day lilies very carefully for colour and time of blooming: earlies, mid-seasons and lates to give bloom throughout July and even later. They thrive in sun but take partial shade with a good grace as does columbine, which will lift your spirits in June. Lobelia and pansies make good companions, and there is lily-of-the-valley if you have a bed where it can spread out to its heart's content, which it will, in shade of course.

And how could I forget hellebores, the Christmas roses? You will want these close to the house and may have to brush the snow off in early March to see their white porcelain blooms.

Colour in August is a problem for any garden and is the time when annuals see us through (impatiens and begonias for the shade gardener) . . . or plants in pots, geraniums and such, which you can lift out into a sunny spot.

If these suggestions are not enough, you could have a look through the catalogues, which often list their 'Plants for Shade' under that heading, and make your own discoveries. Then, in the dog days of summer, you can bask in the envy of all your neighbours who long for just one tree.

If we had stayed in the acid garden, I know I would have tried rhododendron and flaming azaleas. But we didn't stay. Little notes kept appearing about the house: 'Get us out of here.' Some were even attached to the houses-for-sale section of *The Globe and Mail*.

The Tired Garden

Gordon and Elizabeth found the next house. 'It's a little strange,' Gordon said, 'but lots and lots of space.'

'It's beautiful,' cried Elizabeth. 'Oh, please buy it!' We had walked into the second act of *Sleeping Beauty*, which explained Elizabeth's enthusiasm. Cobwebs, a yard long, floated gracefully down over collapsed strips of rather elegant wallpaper. The owner, a charming old gentleman, assured me sadly that it had once been a very happy house.

It was strange, all right. You entered into what had been the hall and faced a graceful, generous staircase. But—and I'm not sure of this—someone had removed the wall between the hall and the living-room, converting an ingle-nook fireplace into half an ingle-nook, which had originally been either in the hall or the living-room. An odd little room led off from the foot of the stairs and had doors, one leading into the garden and another down the back hall past the back door, past the cellar door, past the boot cupboard and eventually into the kitchen. So it hadn't been the butler's pantry. Too far away. If anyone had wanted to convert the place into a rooming house, this odd little room would have been the ideal place to sit and collect the rents as people went in and out. If it had been in the hall, it might have been a cloakroom. If it had been in the living-room, where another door led into the garden . . . ? What was this room meant to be?

As I continued through the three floors on my tour, this question became paramount. Five bedrooms I recognized as what they were. A big study with fireplace on the second floor was clear enough. But across the hall, you went up two steps into a tiny anteroom, which led to a huge triangular glassed-in space, big enough to be a ballroom. But it wasn't.

As I returned to the first floor I came upon a door leading off the staircase landing. Opening this, I was able to plunge down the stairs through a dark tunnel and, with the assistance of three winding treads at the bottom, hurtle head first into the kitchen. This kitchen could have served a restaurant. My heart went out to the first servants in this house, who not only had that stair to contend with but had lived on the third floor with no heat. A later owner, tender of heart, had installed a second furnace and sent the pipes up through the corner of the living-room. They were four inches in diameter and still in full and glorious view.

I said, 'No.'

I said, 'Absolutely not.'

I added, 'Are you both mad?'

Emotion getting me nowhere, I resorted to reason and spelt out the cost of rewiring, new plumbing, new heating. We would have to furnish with orange crates and gingham. How could I decorate rooms when I didn't know what they were? No.

They bought it.

Two months later I sat disconsolate in what was either the hall or the living-room or both, and wondered where to get hold of it when there was a knock at the door. It was Mr. L.

'I'm redecorating the Pattersons' just three doors away and saw your car. Just thought I'd say hello.'

I waved him in. He looked at me. Then he looked around and said, 'Presents problems, doesn't it? Almost insurmountable.' Why that should have cheered me up I don't know, but I was in a weak state and could see he wanted to cheer me up.

We squared our shoulders and toured together, climbing over electricians, carpenters and plumbers, my spirits rising, his descending, and when I at last threw open the door on a small room, which still wore its original whitewash of calcimine, date 1909, he collapsed against the door frame. 'I'm going to have a medal struck for you' was all he said.

What he did, I realize now, was a brilliant stroke of common sense, though at the time it appeared to be madness. He returned in a week, the light of battle in his eye, wearing a confident smile and carrying yards and yards of the Italian silk over his arm. I was speechless while he tossed it up over the old curtain rods and indicated that it was to sweep round both wide bay windows of the living-room, through the hall, and be repeated in the dining-room. A lush broadloom of a slightly deeper colour, in generous sample, dropped to the floor.

'All the living-room?' I had found my voice. He smiled.

'And the hall?' A little nod.

'And up the stairs?'

He never tried to sell you anything or to persuade. He just produced things like a rabbit out of a hat, then watched your face to see if you lit up.

The pipes were already out of sight. A classic column had been in place across one corner of the room. Heaven knows what was behind it. We didn't ask. We just copied it to cover the pipes.

But the kitchen staircase was now out in the open, its canopy removed, and came sensibly down the wall to a sedate little landing and three steps out onto the kitchen floor. It had a neat pine banister.

'Pine for the kitchen cupboards?' asked Mr. L.

'And for the table and chairs and a dresser.'

He held a sample of wallpaper against the pine. The carpenter left his tools to admire and we all said, 'Oooh!' The plumber joined us to see the dining-room paper and we all said, 'Aaah!'

By then I was following Mr. L. down the back hall where the kitchen tile (one of those wipe-off-and-forget-its) was to lead out past the boot cupboard, the back door, the cellar door, and into the little room that led to the garden.

'What *is* this room?' asked Mr. L.

'It might have been a cloakroom,' and I opened the door to the cupboard under the stairs, which would hold three jackets and an umbrella.

'It *is* the cloakroom,' he said. The carpenter was called in and told to build a real coat cupboard along the wall.

I said yes to everything. What he had made me realize was that, once you have taken the plunge, it's no use dithering around and treading water. Confidence is all. The only course is to dive in and thrash your way to shore. I can't say that I realized all this at the time.

The upper floors were furnished with paint and simple cottons. Jon did remark that we could do with more furniture on the upper decks, but he had brought four friends to stay and we ran out of bureau drawers. Elizabeth said, 'You've ruined it. It isn't romantic any more.'

You may wonder why all this talk of houses in a book about gardens, and I will confess that I have now reached an age when my undisciplined brain hares off into the long grass in pursuit of its own interests. It's like walking the dog. However, there is something to be said for taking thought about the house when planning a garden. Actually, it would be better to think about the garden when planning the house. Architects rarely do, and builders and developers never do. Toronto's best districts are chock-a-block with magnificent homes, each set on a lot the size of a tennis court, or perched up in the air on a mole-hill of earth. The effect is ludicrous. I know of two cases where the owners bought the house next door, demolished it, and replaced it with a garden. On that solution, no comment.

Our architectural curiosity had a solution of sorts. It had been angled to meet the sidewalk at the garage end, so allowed space for a flat area of grass, a pretty walk, and two deep flower beds along the face of the house where it turned away from the street. It was still too small and too late to do anything about it. The best answer is to make sure that there is enough land to support the house at the beginning.

The day came when not a sound was to be heard in our house. Even the dust had gone. I stepped out the back door onto a two-foot strip of concrete and smack up against a chain-link fence. On the other side of the fence someone crouched, nicking weeds out of a flower bed. 'Well, you've been busy,' she said, rocking back on her heels. 'The day you moved the coal out, I thought I'd better wait to introduce myself.' This was Nancy F. (My life is blessed with Nancys. What the name means I have no idea, but they are all endowed with common sense to an alarming degree. Nancy C., Elizabeth's godmother, had called around through the winter to sip tea in clouds of plaster dust and say, 'You simply can *NOT* live here.' She restrains me when she can.)

Nancy F. was a gardener, and she was over the fence to assist the moment I asked what the soil was like. A little poking revealed that the soil of my small oasis was quite unlike her garden and stood a good ten inches higher than the three surrounding yards.

'Someone,' said Nancy, 'at sometime, has loaded this space with about two feet of topsoil and now it's packed down.'

'Topsoil? But everything's dead.' I looked at the huge mock orange, its dead leaves spread out to cover the whole width of the back yard. The lilac in the east corner looked no better.

'The soil is old and tired.'

'It's so small. I could rip out the whole area and start again.' Nancy stayed my hand. She persuaded me to saw, cut, and prune the mock orange and lilac, going in on hands and knees, cutting at ground level and tracing the tough old branches up through the tangle, cutting them again and tearing them out until only new young growth remained. This was cut back just enough to give shape and let air through. The day we moved the coal out couldn't even compare. I wore band-aids from head to foot and the front walk was stacked high with brush piles of dead wood, which I had tied and manhandled down the narrow walk. Peat moss, manure and sewage sludge were manhandled into the garden. Compost was started in one small corner and the result of all that was eight-to-ten-foot shrubs scenting the garden and the whole house in a matter of a month. New shrubs would have taken years. In an old garden, stay your hand and see what you can renew and revitalize.

Fragrance belongs in every garden, but a city garden is where it is most needed and appreciated. Mock orange, lilac and roses should be chosen as much for their perfume as their appearance; flowers and herbs as well. Bring them close to your windows and, on a fine spring evening, open the casement. You'll discover what I mean.

A bed under the living-room window was completely empty and on investigation proved to be an excellent candidate for double digging. Instructions for this enterprise are in every gardening book, but in case you have never come across them, here they are. Remove all the topsoil from one section at the left end. Wheel this up to the right or far end. Now return to your first section and with a fork or spade thoroughly loosen the subsoil, digging deep and adding sand if it's clay, humus if it's sand. Well-rotted manure is always a good idea. Now remove the topsoil from the next section and toss it onto the subsoil you have just worked. Continue until you have come to the last section and on this simply unload the wheelbarrow. When I say 'toss the upper soil' I mean just that. Garden beds, like soufflés, need air to perform well. This bed responded to the treatment, supporting grandiflora roses planted in compost. I like tall plants outside a low window: then the flowers can be seen from inside the room.

A large elm grew on Nancy's side of the fence and generously shaded a part of our tiny garden. I saw her one morning standing beneath the tree and gazing up with some concern. Something was eating the leaves. As we watched, the culprit, a small green caterpillar, lowered himself on a long thin thread; then more appeared, enough to convince her that firm action should be taken. A tree firm was called. Their men arrived and sprayed with professional expertise. The caterpillars died, the grass and plants beneath the tree died, and the tree lost most of its leaves. A slight mistake had been made. A residue of weed killer had been in the sprayer.

We now put our heads together. We both had children and pets and so had all the neighbours. We didn't want to use arsenate of lead, Black Leaf 40, or any other lethal mixture, but what to use instead? In those days faint whispers of something called Organic Gardening were about, and I had copied down a recipe for a witches' brew made up of three large onions, one full garlic and a dash of red hot peppers. These went through the blender and were diluted with three quarts of water. After standing overnight, the brew was strained through cheesecloth. You were supposed to spray the juice and bury the mash in the rose bed. We wondered if that would work. With the slugs, aphids and rose-munchers taking over the garden, something stronger seemed to be required. When in doubt, go to the top.

I called the Agricultural Department at the University of Guelph. The young man on the phone began to read off a list of potions that would wipe out the neighbourhood and I hastily explained about the pets and children. 'Ah yes, you don't want me, you want . . . ' He sighed gently and put me through. The new voice, quiet, deliberate and infinitely wise, conjured up a picture of an elderly gentleman isolated in a tower, high above the brisk young men in the laboratories below. Rather like Merlin. I explained our problem.

'Do you have a pen and paper? Very good. Now write this down.' Slowly he spelt out *Bacillus thuringiensis*. It *was* Merlin! This magic spell would wipe out caterpillars and harm nothing else, not even a bee. Unfortunately, it wasn't available in Canada, but would be once tests were complete. (C.I.L. markets it now under the name THURICIDE, better known as Bt.) I asked him about the onion-and-garlic brew for aphids.

'I would try it,' he said, 'Oh yes, I would try it.' He chuckled to himself and wished me goodbye.

When I went out to report, Nancy was dashing back and forth between a rose bed at the end of the drive and another by her kitchen door. 'Come and look!' My turn to climb the fence. The roses by the drive were green with aphids all along the stem. Those by her kitchen door were completely free of them. 'See. It works. Onions work.' And she pointed out two large plants of chives tucked into the kitchen rose bed. *Bacillus thuringiensis* was placed in the garden book for future reference, and, meanwhile, we mixed up our potent brew of onions and garlic. The following afternoon we sprayed it liberally all over her large garden and my small plot. As we finished, her husband swept into the drive, stepped out, and told us in crisp and measured tones that the whole of Rosedale smelt like a pizza parlour, and what were we doing *now*?

The aphids left and the neighbours, when we attempted an apology, said they were leaving too, for their summer cottages. Everything left but the slugs. For these, we tried poison bait under rocks, until we realized we were attracting all the slugs for miles around. Wood ashes worked better.

Now Roy E. Biles emerged from his hiding place at the back of the shelves because I was going to plant a lot of tulips across the front of the house and I wanted to do it right. Mr. Biles was as forthright as ever. Excavate the entire bed. To what depth? There had to be nine to ten inches of soil from the point of the bulb up. (These were big three-inch bulbs.) So that was twelve inches, and they should sit on a bed of sand two inches deep. Once I had excavated the entire bed to fourteen inches and the sand had arrived, we all had to go in and out the back door for a week. While I was smoothing and levelling the sand, a courtly gentleman paused to say that he had been observing me for some time and, though he hadn't yet decided whether I was a good gardener, he had no doubt whatsoever at all but that I was a formidable gardener. Then the postman, on his daily rounds, handed me some letters, gazed into the pit and said, 'You'll never see them again—they're too deep.'

I was now placing them on the sand as directed, in big circles of a dozen to each clump. The soil was mixed with bone meal and wood ash on the front walk (the whole enterprise was a disgrace to the neighbourhood) and at last shovelled back in and watered.

We saw them again, year after year, great golden globes, never seeming to split or grow smaller. They survived annuals planted and removed from above. They even survived the small boys who had discovered that, if they lit a firecracker tucked inside a bloom, they could achieve a magnificent display. So *Garden Magic* was right again. The postman never said a word.

We had wonderful years in that house. Rooms that have no particular purpose never stand empty. Everyone should have a kitchen stair. It's a great place to sit and talk, sit and eat, or sit and toss comment down to those who are at the kitchen table. It was here that the great project of the Grub Street Banana Band was hatched and the decision made to rehearse in the glassed-in room over the garage. Unacquainted with rock 'n' roll, Gordon and I now had some qualms as we saw the amplifiers moved in, but we had given permission and that was that. The first rehearsal we thought would be the last as the house lights rose and fell in rhythm with the drum, to which they had attached a light, and we waited for the phone to ring. It did. The neighbours were complaining. Would we please open the windows? They couldn't hear. I pleaded for the peace and sanity of the elderly lady across the street. Well then, could they come in and sit on the stairs?

I glanced out the back window and saw Nancy's husband standing out on the grass and looking up at the windows. I went out to receive his complaints, but he called, 'Hey! They're good!' I don't know. They must have been. They thrived for two years and made a handsome profit, but their last years at university were looming. Life was real, life was earnest, and they folded the band.

Time was marching for us all. Jon came home from Syracuse with his Master's degree and a bright yellow car, loaded it up with all his worldly goods, and took off to CFPL-TV in London, Ontario, for his first full-time job. David came home with his Bachelor's degree and a bright yellow knapsack. Lugging a tape recorder as well, he was setting off for Europe. When he got to Stockholm he would drop in and visit Elizabeth, who was now in her second year with the Royal Swedish Ballet.

The house was empty.

It was then I heard from the elderly lady across the street. 'My dear, I hope you won't think me intrusive, but I had to ask. What has happened to the lovely music? And all the children in their funny clothes?'

When I told her, she sighed and said, 'Oh dear, I do miss them.' I missed them too.

Who taught us to face facts? I am old enough now to know what a futile occupation that is. If you wait, they change into new facts. If you ignore them, they go away. A friend suggested that we close off the third floor and that would leave us with just three bedrooms, two dens and the main floor, the best advice we've ever had. But we faced facts. We went looking for the perfect retirement home for an elderly couple and found it.

On moving day, for the first time, I walked through the empty rooms of a house, reluctant to leave. We had put our roots down in this rambling, quirky old place.

David had said, 'How could you? Oh, how could you?' when we sold it.

'But you moved out.'

'What's that got to do with it?'

Now I leaned a forehead against the cold pane of the window. The garden was under snow. Thin tubes of ice outlined the branches of mock orange and lilac, sparkling in the sun. The roses were tucked up in their winter cover. I knew where the winter aconites would unfold through the snow come spring, right beside the cold frame. The delphiniums were in there, fattening up. Would the new owner remember to thin the mock orange, know how to prune the roses? Don't even think about it. I knew that some gardeners take a plant or two or a cutting to the new house. Would I? Even if I could? Everything was comfortably asleep and, for that matter, frozen in tight, safe and sound. Why disturb it? Make a clean break. Let it go.

At the new house I dried my tears, wandered to the front window, and looked out at the pretty little house behind the pretty little picket fence across the street. A road ran down beside it and at the entrance to the road was a large sign: it said DEAD END.

NOTES FOR THE NOVICE

Bulbs

NARCISSUS (Daffodils)

These will divide and increase on their own. Yellow or white, they lift their trumpets to the sky or shyly hang their heads. Save the expensive species to give your borders vibrant colour in the spring. Cheaper collections, which often contain beautiful surprises, can be drifted out into long grass, meadows, or open woods.

To plant, use a spade. Plant shallow if you want them to spread. Cover with soil three times the height of the bulb to hold them to size. Make the hole wide enough to plant groups of at least a dozen, 4 to 6 inches (10–15 cm) apart.

TULIPS

You don't want tulips to divide, so plant them deeply. (See p. 43.) I count on four to five years of bloom from mine. Bone meal and wood ashes go in below the bulbs when they are planted, followed by a yearly feeding thereafter. Go to all lengths to get the colour you want and the date of blooming, taking into account the colour of shrubs if these are blooming nearby.

Ensure that you will have delivery before the ground freezes. One friend stored a hundred bulbs in the refrigerator until March, then planted and had bloom that year. One November we cut through two inches of ice and planted seven hundred bulbs into the cold, cold ground. They bloomed triumphantly the following spring. The bulbs won't mind the cold but you will, so plead for delivery in October.

SMALL BULBS

Crocus, snowdrops, tulipa tarda, sweet-scented jonquil, eranthis (winter aconite), muscari (grape hyacinth), ixiolirion——you will find the list is endless in any good bulb catalogue. Plant these little charmers in the grass, at the edge of borders, or tuck them in close to the door where the snow first melts, just to let you know winter is over . . . well, almost. Most will divide, spread and amble about on their own. Undemanding and faithfully reappearing, they are your garden's best friends.

A good supplier will enclose planting directions with your order. Read and follow faithfully. (I had one bulb that had to be planted on its side!) And don't forget forget-me-not or arabis to accompany the bulbs.

RIPENING

After blooming, it is of the utmost importance to allow the leaves of tulips and daffodils to die down to a limp brown before you remove them. It is during this die-down period that a new flower is forming in the bulb for next year. If you wish to move them to make room for annuals, you must lift the bulbs with leaves still attached, place them in a trench with leaves above ground and let them die down the same way. (It really is easier to leave them in place, as your spade or fork will cut the bulbs and the following autumn, planting time, you will be hard put to it to find the bulbs.)

The Plastic Garden

Gordon didn't like the new house, but he didn't say anything. I didn't like the new house, and I didn't say anything. But when you have been married for years and years, you have to be careful what you think. The other one knows. We sat quietly reading and Gordon said, 'Stop worrying and fidgeting.' I hadn't moved a muscle in an hour. He sat immovable for two and I said, 'If you're going to be this restless, we'd better go on a trip or something.'

What was the matter with the place? I called Bob and Howard, who have painted nearly every house we've ever owned, and they did their level best to re-create the colour scheme of the old house. They even threw in a burnt-orange lining to the kitchen cupboards. 'Cheer you up,' Howard said. Now, how did he know?

Then Bob made the horrifying discovery. 'Something's sticking up out of the snow.' Investigation revealed plastic tulips in the flower beds and plastic daffodils collapsed in the window boxes.

Jon came home for the weekend and after dinner went for a walk. He came home and sat down for a serious talk. 'You two have moved into a retirement village. Everyone I met was over eighty. You don't belong here. Move.'

An old friend came for the evening and at last I asked him, 'What is the matter with this house?'

He looked doubtful, rubbed his knees for a bit, then said, 'I wouldn't say this if you didn't already know. But you do know. It's a mean little house.'

None of this was exactly cheering.

As soon as the snow was gone, the window boxes were pried off and hurled with great joy into the front yard. All the plastic flowers were gathered and thrown out. And on an early June morning we went out to survey the house from the street. There it sat, faintly embarrassed, up on its little mound of earth. What is it with all these hillocks, humps and knolls that builders indulge in? Something to do with drainage or high, dry basements? What a nonsense!

We couldn't lower the house, but we could flatten the lawn from sidewalk to house. Then what? A long, low grey stone wall to tie the house to the ground.

While we thought about it, a small, bright orange cat appeared at our feet. Once he had our attention, he went into his act, performing astounding feats of acrobatics. We asked the girl next door who owned him and she told us he had been dumped from a car and was starving; the neighbours were thinking of calling the Humane Society. The cat ran up a tree and down again, chased his tail and stopped in front of us, ears pricked forward, waiting for applause. He might be starving but he wouldn't beg. A really spunky littly guy.

'George,' we said, 'this is your house,' picked him up, and carried him indoors. George was a businessman, out first thing in the morning to assist the postman, back for a brief lunch, then out again in the afternoon to supervise the team of gardeners who attended to all the gardens along the pretty street. George introduced me to Walter.

We had consulted a landscape firm, who had given us a graph drawing and suggested converting the hump to a long, dreary slope, a few evergreens and a fierce estimate. We decided to forget about it.

It was August when the gardening team arrived next door; and I could see George up a tree, patting at the pruning shears as they snipped, and generally making a nuisance of himself. I went out to collect him.

'This is some cat you have here,' said a big man with a big smile. 'No, leave him alone. We like him.' Then he said, 'I hear you don't like plastic daffodils.' This was Walter.

I told him I didn't like houses on humps either, and he strolled over to have a look.

Walter didn't—and still doesn't—use graph paper. His hand

drew a line across the base of the house. 'It needs a low, grey stone wall about ten feet out to give you a good landing to the front door. Flowers along the top of the wall. An evergreen here and two there.' The hands indicated the evergreens, two fat and round and one tall. 'That anchors the house to the landing. Soften the angle of the wall there with shrubs. Now just take the grass level from the sidewalk to the wall and get rid of that walk. It cuts the lawn in two. We'll cover those concrete side steps with flagstone.' His whole plan and his estimate had me nodding in agreement. How soon?

'Oh, about a week.'

I thought he meant he would start in a week. He meant he would finish in a week. And he did. On the last day he drove around all the markets to find plants and came back with a truck-load. In half an hour the top of the wall was thick with chrysanthemums in bloom, and one long wavy flower bed was crammed with colour.

The lady with the picket fence came over. 'It's been like a play. I haven't done a thing all week but stand at the window and watch. We're so grateful.' So were we. Now we had a pretty garden too. Or rather, we had a garden in front. The back was the usual oblong of grass with a border of indifferent shrubs around the three sides. Two rose beds, six by two feet, side by side in the middle of the lawn, looked all too much like graves. I decided to do a little experimenting on my own and purchased individual plants, primroses, violets, tiny English daisies, and put them in the back border. They were not at all pleased about their new home. I asked Walter about it and he came around the back to see what the problem was. One look and he started to laugh. 'They're all alone! They can't live alone. I'll bring them some company.' And so boxes of primroses, daisies and what-not arrived and were planted in little colonies where they gossiped together, nodded their heads and bloomed. Lilac replaced the shrubs that had come out of the bush up north and would have been happier left where they had been born. Now Walter surveyed the rose beds. 'Let's move those and grass it over.' He walked over to the northeast corner of the garden, turned around, and transformed himself into an ornamental crabapple, arms out and hands drooping, heavy with bloom. 'We'll plant the roses in front of this tree.' I have since seen him turn himself into everything from a multi-trunked maple to a hawthorn. If ever you played 'statues' as a child, you'll have the idea. When in doubt as to what you want to order—a vase shape, a globe or a spreading locust—commandeer members of the family and stand them about the garden in the suitable poses. Of course, you'll have to go through it all over again when the trees arrive, but at least you should have the right-shaped tree in the right place.

Now that we had the garden to cheer us and George to amuse us, we felt we could settle down for a few years; but it was not to be. Overnight, George was gone. Everyone, including the postman, searched for him, and in three days we learned he had been killed by a passing car.

Shortly after this a friend asked if I liked our new house and I shook my head but should have known better—the friend was Jackie, the best real-estate saleswoman in town. Two days later our house was sold. There were tears again, but not for the house. Only for George.

We had three months to find a place to live. Jackie wanted us to rent and take a year to really find the right house. Advice flowed in from all sides. Two friends of long standing, Mary and Jo, found me at the hairdresser's and, as *they* had just moved to the country, *that* was the thing to do. While Gene combed me out, they moved in on either side and started a soft sales pitch.

'It's so quiet.'

'They're lonely,' said Gene.

'The air is clean.'

'Full of mosquitoes,' said Gene.

'We can all grow old together,' murmured Jo in her smoky voice, making it sound like something you might want to do.

'Seriously,' cried Mary, 'You'll love it. And anyway, why are you putting her off, Gene? You're moving out there yourself.'

'Don't do it!' cried Gene. Mary had just sold him a dear little log cabin on six acres and he was now spending sleepless nights and quantities of money trying to make it liveable.

'It's all right, Gene,' said, I. 'We're city people. Not a chance, though of course we would love to drive out next Saturday just for a visit.

'No!' cried Gene. 'Don't. Don't do it!'

Meanwhile, Jackie drove me about to see houses built with side-hall plan and centre-hall plan and finally asked, 'Do you really know what you want? If you don't think about it, you'll just keep moving.'

I found a drawing-board and large sheets of paper in Gordon's den and plonked them down on the living-room floor. I was going to find out what I wanted.

Now, if the subject of houses bores you, you may skip the next bit. I made small cut-outs to scale of the furniture I wanted. Some of it we owned. Some we didn't. But paper doesn't cost anything. The cut-outs were placed on a blank piece of paper so the family and/or guests would be seated at a comfortable distance for conversation but without crowding. Then the fireplace should be there. And I drew it in. And the big window should be here. And I drew it in along with a wide entrance door. When that was all settled, I drew in the walls. Result: one room, twenty-two by twenty.

The dining-room and kitchen were plotted separately the same way. When the three rooms were slid around in different relationships, a floor plan appeared that gave me two small halls. These would act as sight and sound locks between living-room and kitchen. The pattern also produced a fourth room. This was obviously the entrance room—not a hall, but a room with fireplace, outlined with book shelves, a staircase up one wall, and space for fifteen people to arrive all at once, shedding coats and boots, without running up and down each other's backs. *That* was what I wanted.

A sheet of tracing paper over this main floor revealed where the bearing walls would have to be, and that produced four bedrooms and two and a half bathrooms. Each bedroom was planned so that the beds would all have their heads against an inside wall, which is my contribution to the cure for the common cold. One bathroom had a tub, which was deep, long, and wide, with no provision for flappy shower curtains. The other had a shower stall you could walk around in. Now who said I didn't know what I wanted?

If ever you decide to build, try planning from the inside out. Architects are interested in what a house looks like from the outside. The family want a home they can live *in*. My daughter thinks every home should have two doors you can slam, one for him and one for her.

But of course we weren't going to build. Too expensive. Gordon and Jon looked over the plan and sighed deeply. It was folded up and put away in a desk drawer to be forgotten.

We had spent the summer visiting our friends in the country and looking at a few tumble-down farmhouses with Mary. At each of these, I had quietly taken up a fistful of earth and watched the sandy stuff blow away in the wind. At Gene's place, the earth was a deep, dark loam. The only deep, dark stuff *we* could find was inside an immense barn. The barn would convert beautifully, they said. This stall could be the dining-room and that the kitchen, and look up at the old beams. It was when we looked down that I lost courage, and we told Mary we were going to buy in the city. She was off to Florida for the winter and said Sally would look after us if anything turned up. We forgot all about that too.

NOTES FOR THE NOVICE

GOOD SOIL: Rich brown, not black. It feels soft, clings together lightly when squeezed and has no odour of chemicals. If it feels gritty, it contains too much sand. Feel it and smell it before you buy.

CLAY SOIL: Grey, yellow or rust in colour, sticky when wet, and hard when dry. Double- or triple-dig, mixing with sand, humus, compost, or fresh hot horse manure (you will have to let this overwinter before planting). Coarse gravel below for drainage.

SANDY SOIL: Add thoroughly moistened peat moss and all the compost you can make. In an open bed where you can till— *green manure*. That means seeding with buckwheat, rye and clover. Before these flower, till them down and repeat the seeding, growing and tilling until you have good soil. Buckwheat will choke out twitch and weeds. Sand needs the addition of live material, i.e., compost or green manure.

ACID SOIL: You can modify with lime or you can count your blessings and go with what you have, planting the beautiful acid-loving plants: rhododendron, azalea, heather, etc.

STONY SOIL: Till up rocks and remove with stone rake. Frost will continue to lift rocks to the surface, but some left in the soil will do no harm if you build the beds high with good soil, 10 inches (25 cm) or more. Raised beds and some rock below will give you excellent drainage.

Correct the condition of the soil before the plants go in. Saves heart-aches, back-aches, time and money.

II

The Country House

*"Never spoil a good story
for the sake of the truth"*

— ADVICE FROM MY FATHER

Choose the Site with Care

The biggest investment you will ever make is in your home, and there are certain questions you should ask yourself. Is it in a good district? Are good schools close by? Is the price right? Will your bank manager approve? I found all that in a magazine article. Shortly after, we found the house that answered yes to all of the above. So we decided to buy it. We didn't care if we ever saw it again, but we decided to buy it.

Then Sally phoned: 'I've found your land!'

'What?'

'Your land, I've found it! Hills rolling to the south, a woods, a stream—the view is—'

'Sally? Sally. Do listen. We're buying in the city. You see, we have to be sensible—'

'Ah nooo,' and she sounded as if all her heart was in it. This girl could sell. 'If you could see—I know it's yours, I just know it—come and see—'

The gist of all this was passed on to Gordon, and he said, 'She's gone to a lot of trouble. The least we can do is look and then say no.'

As we set out for the country it was snowing lightly, and by the time we got there it was snowing heavily. There was a discussion about going in by skidoo, but as I was wearing the only warm coat I owned, a new mink, a chic little hat and thin leather knee-high boots, Sally looked me up and down and said we would drive in. The car careened skittishly along the gravel roads and in a final flourish, slid around a curve, fish-tailed up onto a track on the side of a hill and stopped.

'This is the Winter Road,' they said.

We climbed to the top of the next hill. They showed me how to do a herringbone, ski-style, toes out, heels in (high heels are a great help). Then we went over the top of the ridge and slid down waist-deep in snow. The sky had turned black. A gale-force wind whipped snow and trees and clouds. Hills did indeed roll away to the south, with pastures, meadows, valleys of trees, tiny little inch-high houses making an unbelievable picture all the way to the horizon, all the way to Toronto, fifty miles away. Five hundred thousand acres of it.

'This is one good site for the house,' they said.

Then they said, 'You'll have to fall over.'

That seemed like a good idea, but what they meant was that you couldn't pull your legs out of snow that deep. The technique is to pitch forward on your stomach and then swim and claw your way onto the surface.

Memory fails as to how we got to the woods. I can recall following a small stream through the frozen snow with soaking wet feet and coming out of the cedar swamp onto higher ground. The ground rose and rose until we were surrounded by the biggest beech trees I had ever seen, sugar maples and spruce, until we were at last face to face with an insurmountable hill. We surmounted it. On our stomachs we snaked up, feet slithering as footholds gave way. As we came into the clearing on top, we faced another panorama of hills and sky.

'Or you could build the house here,' they said.

In silence we departed for Toronto. Still in silence we had our dinner. After dinner I sat gazing at the newspaper held firmly up in front of Gordon's face.

'Are you thinking what I'm thinking?'

The newspaper came down. 'Buy it,' he said.

'Then we can build that house,' he added, 'and you can have a country garden.' He didn't have to persuade me.

Jon was appalled. 'I didn't mean you were to go back to the land! *Back* to it? You've never been *on* it!'

Jon was right, of course. He frequently is. We were within puffing distance of our sixties, knew nothing about the district or what it would cost, and had gone against all the advice of the experts; we had bought a view. We knew that. What we didn't know was that we had bought a complete new life-style, moved onto another planet and, most desperate of all, purchased the site for a garden under five feet of snow.

But in one sense we had chosen the site with care. We cared! We had to have it. We couldn't say no. Blinded by wind and slightly concussed, not in our right minds, we had bought a view of acres and acres of land we would never own. We had chosen the place we would call home for years to come, and I hope you find your own true love too. When you do, you won't ask a lot of silly questions.

No Problem

Once the papers, all in order, were back from the lawyer, we found that we had purchased twenty acres in the Township of Mono, Dufferin County. Dufferin County is north and west of Toronto and is referred to as 'the roof of Ontario'. The Niagara Escarpment runs through it. Ranging from 1400 to 1750 feet above sea level, this undulating plateau in the sky contains marsh areas where the Grand River, the Humber and the Nottawasaga have their headwaters.

'Mono' we first pronounced with a short 'o', as in 'monster', but were firmly corrected by the more elderly locals. 'Moe-noe' they would intone every time we made the slip. There are many charming tales as to how the name originated, but the most likely is that it comes from the Gaelic *monadh*, which means hill. It was settled by the Irish coming in shortly after the 1820 survey of the land, some by wagon, some by boat up-river; and a great number walked in.

Their descendants are still here. At least twenty in our small township live in the houses their forebears built, serving on the Mono or Dufferin Councils as their fathers and grandfathers did. Believe me, they know the territory. These are our neighbours and friends, along with city people such as ourselves, a liberal sprinkling of Dutch, German, English, new Irish, boat people. All the new-comers are in the process of learning, just as the later pioneers learned from the first-comers, how to cope with the land, the weeds, the wind, the snow, the power blackouts and, most important of the lot, how to drive on ice!

The history of Dufferin is amusingly and accurately told in Adelaide Leitch's book *Into the High County*. *Yellow Briar*, mostly fact, partly fiction, is charmingly told by Paddy Slater, who was really John Mitchell. His home, the Yellow Briar, is still here, along with the old coaching inns (converted to restaurants), the tiny churches, the log cabins, the old one-room schools (converted into homes) and, alas, only some of the original stores on Broadway in Orangeville.

I can't leave this subject without mentioning the Indians. Originally, this was the land of the Petun, but by the time the settlers came the inhabitants were the Ojibwa. Our small personal patch was a part of the Ojibwa hunting ground. In their day the Humber was a deep river, and our woods held pools and ponds and a lively stream (now a trickle), which would have held trout. They must have known, as we do now, where the ginger root grows on the bank above the spring and where the wild asparagus and jack-in-the-pulpit flourish. I sometimes wonder: did they encourage all those pesky edible greens that do so well in my vegetable garden? On a snowy night I picture them out there in their tipis. My husband says they're fine, they have a fire. The whole place seems a long, long way from Holt Renfrew.

All this information was a part of the future. All we knew as we left the plastic garden was that we owned a mysterious twenty acres somewhere north of Toronto. But I, at least, was bursting with confidence. We had the plan for the house. I knew what to do with whatever soil we found, be it clay or sand, sweet or sour. I knew the plants I wanted. And I had Walter. Gordon was starting a new company, so it was high hopes all round as we sailed up the Airport Road 'all in the blue, unclouded weather'. As the young today so blithely put it, 'no problem'.

I had phoned Sally and asked her if she could find us a nice place to live near our land, so that we could study it once the snow melted. Everything had to be planned down to the last foot and firmly plotted on graph paper before one workman was allowed near the place. 'That's the first thing we should do,' I said.

Sally said, 'The first thing you should do is buy a pair of skidoo boots, $8.95, and a padded ski jacket, $23.95. You can get them out here at Norman's.' As an afterthought she added, 'I'll find you a place to live.' The place she found was a small white farmhouse next to a large cow barn on the 5th sideroad.

The entire family was now converging on the place. Jon was driving in from London; David, in a white panel truck, was on the long trek from Vancouver, through the Rockies, the plains and the forests, coming home. Liz had packed her trunks for the last time and said a last farewell to Sweden, and was about to put down at Toronto International. Why were they all coming home? No one said. They gave various personal reasons, but we rather suspected their confidence in our project was less firm than ours. But the day came when we were able to take them over to see the land and let them wander about into the woods and up onto the ridge to see the view, and we were at last faced with three identical grins. The verdict was yes. No problem.

The Well-Laid Plans

We didn't put a foot wrong. Our architect came highly recommended. We had seen his restoration work at two houses
and loved it. So that was all right.

We checked out three builders and chose the one who came
recommended by a real-estate agent and a bank manager. We
looked over a house he had built, admired the joinery, the
straight walls, the installation of the tile. That was all right.

We paid a lawyer to search the title on our land and a surveyor
to survey it.

Older residents in the area gave us excellent advice. Anyone
building in the country must, absolutely must, drill the well first
and get the road in. There were horror stories in abundance: of
the man who built first and then proceeded to drill five dry
wells, of roads that became impassable for half the year, were
too steep or too low and drifted in with snow, of houses too
close to the main road, so that dust blew in with every passing
car. We took note. The road would go in first and then the well.
Everything was under control.

As for the garden, the architect had the best idea of all: pop
the house down on the site we had chosen and leave the wildflowers to grow. He told us about the daisies, the Indian paint-
brush, the blue chicory, the Queen Anne's lace of summer and
the purple asters of fall. All we would want was a small vegetable garden and one or two flower beds. No grass. Who wants
to spend the idle days of summer cutting grass?

More than that, we had a full winter in the white farmhouse
to work out details. How could anything go wrong?

We stayed a year in the farmhouse. All five of us had fallen
on it with buckets of suds. Such energy amazed our landlord
and he joined the party, installing a new kitchen sink, remod-
elling the bathroom and two bedrooms. Then he insisted on

hooking up my washer and dryer. We thought we'd have our own house built before he finished. Mary and Jo, with husbands, the friends who had lured us out to the country, would come whizzing by to assure us that we would soon be out of all this, wrinkling up their fastidious noses.

But we loved the farm. So what if there were forty-four cows in the neighbouring barn, all of them pregnant? It enlivened the nights. Cows are not stoic when in the throes of parturition. After one such night, I came down at five in the morning to make myself a cup of tea and, as I sipped it, I gazed out the window at the mist swirling in great scarves over the fields. A black shape with far too many legs appeared, was lost, and reappeared to reveal itself as one cow and one just-born calf standing nose to nose in astonishment. As it was her first calf and obviously his first mother, they had much to be surprised about. I was surprised too. They both knew exactly what to do, though no one had taught them how.

As well as producing calves, the cows produced quantities of manure. When the landlord's son, Roger, observed me freeing up the old peonies in the yard and loosening the soil in the narrow bed that surrounded the house, like his father, he couldn't do enough for me. So, while I was out, he took the front-end loader and stacked manure fresh from the cow all around the house, two feet deep.

Elizabeth and I were overwhelmed. We couldn't breathe.

His father was enraged. 'I ask you to do something nice for her. So what do *you* do?' He raised both fists to the sky and his voice to the stratosphere. 'YOU BURY HER IN COW-SH—' He bit off the word and all but caught his tongue. This effort at restraint had the veins standing out on his brow and his son rocking helplessly on the tractor. Elizabeth and I were trying not to laugh; when you laugh you breathe in. At last Roger turned to me, tears in his eyes, and said, 'It's to make your flowers grow.'

'Oh, Roger! I'll explain later,' and we took off hastily for Orangeville, leaving father and son to sort it out.

Fresh, hot whatever-you-want-to-call-it will burn and destroy anything you plant in it. I thought everyone knew that, but learned in the years to follow that though the farmers know the meaning of rotted and well-rotted manure, many of their sons do not. Some part of this I explained to Elizabeth as we rolled along number 9 to town.

The last time we had shopped together had been in Paris, on the rue du Faubourg St. Honoré. In less than an hour we had decided that Broadway in Orangeville was infinitely superior. Besides, we could afford it. On the main street of most small country towns, you can start with a list that includes mouse-traps, odd bits of hardware, a nut to fit this bolt, knitting wool, the groceries, a pair of jeans, a call at the bank, a note to see the lawyer, and at the end of two blocks it's done. Then, well satisfied, you can pop into a tearoom and have a coffee with a home-baked biscuit and strawberry jam.

More than that, you nose your car in to the front of each store, cross the sidewalk and walk in. If the article is heavy, they put it in the car for you. If they can't find it, they say, 'Wait a minute', run down to the basement and find it.

We all liked this life. Though they weren't living with us, one or the other of the children, or all three with friends, came for weekends. Gene was just up the road in his refurbished log cabin, and he and Joe would wine and dine us in front of the great fieldstone fireplace, which filled most of one wall.

As I looked at the new-turned earth in his garden and played around with the de-manured beds at the farm, I just couldn't wait to be starting on my own property, digging into this lush dark earth.

But all that had to wait. Nothing could happen until we had the blueprint. Rather than hold long explanatory conversations, we had simply handed over the plan that had been tucked into the deep desk drawer. Our plan was drawn to scale, including the four elevations, but the roof was too high. 'Change the roof but don't change the floor plan, not by one square inch.' The architect nodded his assent and smiled.

We were all there when Gordon brought home the profes-sional plans. They were rolled out on the floor and we all knelt round on the rug. There was the front elevation, complete with a non-existent tree. Never mind. What an enchanting house! We flipped over the first page to the main floor plan, full of anticipation. But there'd been a mistake. It wasn't our house. Our name was on the plan, but it wasn't our house. It wasn't our house at all.

It's an old story: the architect wants to design *his* house and you want him to design *your* house. I explained that I understood this, that I would just go quietly away, but instead he swore I could have what I wanted, and we moved into a love-hate relationship: a tug of war, as he pushed walls in and I pushed them back out. We were both properly brought up and we were polite, then very polite, then coldly polite until we ended up head-on about the staircase. He wanted it to come straight down the wall, ending up at the hall cupboard, and I wanted it to turn into the front room.

'Why?' We were standing knee-deep in grass in our field for this argument.

'Because,' I said, 'I'm going to have a party and the ladies are going to arrive in very beautiful and expensive dresses. They'll go upstairs and leave their coats, then descend the stairs, come to the landing, turn, and make a graceful entrance into the room where their admiring husbands are standing by the bar.' My voice rose in rage and disbelief. 'You want them to end up in the hall cupboard?'

He shouted with laughter. 'I don't believe it! You really mean it!' After that, things got better. The outside walls could adjust themselves to the rooms we wanted inside and not the other way around. When you see your blueprint, get inside it and walk around, cook, take a bath, hold a dinner party, take the kids' snowboots off, do the washing. Can you live in it? That's what matters.

So I lost a few battles and won the war. And so did he. He gave the house an ambiance and a warmth I could never have mastered, he raised the ceilings, pulled down the roof, added grace and charm. Now all we had to do was build it.

The Battle of the Blueprint had started in February, two

months before we moved to the farm in early April. We had hoped to start building in late May, as soon as the frost was out of the ground, but the arguments and the days had dragged on to mid-June. So the first of July was set as the starting date. Two days before we were to break ground, the builder called to say that two feet had been taken off the front room in the last drawing, and I wouldn't be able to get the piano in. 'Don't wait for them!' he shouted. 'You change the plan!'

I called the draughtsman and asked if he would re-draw the basement if I did the first and second floors. At first he said he would, but in ten minutes he called back to tell me he had just found the original set of *my* plans. 'They're great,' said he. 'Solves all our problems. Everything will fit. If you'll wait three days, I'll give you a whole new set of blueprints to *your* plan.'

'You've never seen them before?'

'Nope. Just found them.'

'It's taken five months to get the blueprint I have now.'

'Please. I promise you. Just three days.'

I made the worst decision I have ever made in my life. I said no.

If there is one thing a gardener should have it is patience, and it is needed in the planning and construction of a house far more than it is in a garden, which is amenable to some alteration. Dig in your heels and wait it out until you get what you want—though I admit that it is difficult to do. In our case, there was barely time to get the house closed in before winter, and I didn't believe the three days. We re-drew the front room, pushing the wall back out, and went with what we had.

The house had been staked out on the first plateau where we had stood waist-deep in snow. It was oriented so that the big living-room window caught the view, and the first ridge we had climbed extended like a long arm to cradle the house on the northeast from wind and weather. On the appointed day we met there with the builder and the 'dozer man. He was shown where to cut the drive through the depression between two hills, which were a blaze of blue and gold flowers in the tall green grass. The drive was to swing out in a circle in front of the house, and any topsoil was to be stacked in the centre. Ah yes, and the septic tank would be to the west. Then we left him to it.

Don't ever do that. Not with a bulldozer. Stay right there with a loud-hailer and a gun. When we returned the next day, he had skinned off two acres and was still there. 'Took off all your weeds!' he called. Indeed, at great risk to life and limb, he had manoeuvered that immense machine on a slant up the sides of the hills and peeled everything off. Goodbye Plan One for garden.

Jon kept a photographic record of the building of the house and mounted the product in an album for me, leaving the right-hand pages blank. 'That's so you can write the story,' he said. No, I can't live through all that again, not even on paper. It started well. The footings, concrete block and framing were well done by skilled teams of work people, but they were followed by strange crews who obviously didn't know what they were about. And the builder was seldom there. Time revealed that he had paid a commission to the man who recommended him, owed money to the bank manager and had not built the house he was using as a sample of his work. Obviously, one should not only get references but should get references with reference to the references. Other clients of his came to us, wild-eyed, begging us to join them and sue. But adding lawyers to our cast of characters we felt would lead to utter bedlam.

Construction at the house was going from bad to worse. Calamity was hard on the heels of Disaster, but help was at hand; the Lord moves in mysterious ways. Hydro went on strike and there was no power. The bricklayers went on strike and other trades walked out in sympathy. Now nothing at all was happening at the house, and that was a tremendous improvement.

As soon as the power went off, we had moved in an industrial heater to keep the drying plaster gently warm, and someone had to be around to keep an eye on it. The builder answered an ad in a local paper and hired a freelance carpenter. George, his name was, and, as he was local, I made a few enquiries. 'If he's in the mood, you couldn't find a better man' was the verdict. Keeping George in a good mood was simply a case of giving him good-quality material to work with.

I handed him my scale drawings for the panelling and bookcases round the front-room fireplace and for the kitchen.

'Can you work from these, George?'

'Have to be a damn fool if I couldn't,' said George. He was there alone all day, working slowly and lovingly, fitting precisely, and taking great pleasure in using the lengths of custom trim left over from the window mouldings and the baseboards. I would drive over through the softly falling snow and together we would talk over which piece looked best where. None of this slap-it-together stuff for George. Ingenious was what he was.

Meanwhile, back at the farm, we were deep in snow. The landlord came in for a chat one evening, and as he and Gordon were talking, a small strange crying noise caught my attention. It went on and on, and when I opened the front door a great whoosh of snow and a small ugly cat blew in together. She whizzed past me into the sitting-room, straight for Gordon, and, leaping into his lap, placed a paw on either shoulder, looked frantically up into his face and cried, 'Save me! Save me!' It was all I could do to get her away from him to feed her. We couldn't throw her back into the storm, so she stayed overnight. The landlord assured me that none of the neighbours owned her.

In the morning I put her out to find her way home. An hour later I opened the front door and there she was, ears pricked proudly forward, and lying on the concrete step was an immense and very dead rat. This was not greeted with joyful cries. The following morning she brought five mice, laid out like neat little exclamation marks on the same step. This time I had the courtesy to say thank you.

Of course we brought her in out of the storm at night and of course we took her to the vet and of course we bought her a

litter box and a fetching little basket bed as a coming-home present. The landlord said, 'Looks as if you've got yourself a cat.
What are you going to call her?'

'Miranda.'

David said it meant 'a wonder of a girl'. Whatever it meant,
we began to suspect that she thought she was a dog. The only
animal she would tolerate was the landlord's old black mongrel.
If the crew of cats from the barn came over, she raised her hack-
les and growled. Most of them tortoise-shell as she was and
every bit as ugly, they were obviously her original family, but
she was cutting them dead.

I was a little miffed that Gordon should be the object of her
undying love while I was just the character who put the food
out and said *no*. She didn't like the word, but she obeyed it.
Determined to move up in the world with her own bed and her
own powder room, she took to manicuring her claws only on
the outside fence posts and her dog-like characteristics began
to fade. She was fast becoming Gordon's girlfriend and my
social secretary, greeting one and all at the door. Gene had two
pure-breds, one all black and one a pearl grey, who wore dia-
mante collars, but he thought our barn cat had the same elegant
manners. 'Barn' was another word that laid her ears back. No
reference to her lowly beginnings, if you please! We had ourselves a cat all right, that is, if she really was a cat.

What with George at the house and Miranda at the farm, the
days mosied along peacefully, but I had a problem to solve.
Between the second and first floors of the house there was only
a rickety ladder nailed at both ends. The builder at last confessed that he didn't know what to do about it. He usually
installed pre-fabricated metal, he said. So I called a firm recommended by the architect.

A bright, noisy, cheerful little man came to see me at the
house, whipped off his coat, produced a tape measure and
measured. Looking doubtful, he measured again and then said,
'Can't do it.'

'What? Can't do what?'

'Can't get a staircase in here. No room.

Briskly he showed me that, if we took it straight down the wall, it would end up eighteen inches from the cupboard door and seal off the entrance to the dining-room. If we turned it as the blueprint showed, it would take a foot off the dining-room entrance. My beautiful ladies would have to sidle in sideways. Once he could see that I was convinced, he waved a cheerful goodbye.

George came slowly in from the kitchen and we stood gazing silently at the hole in the ceiling and the hole in the floor.

'Will you let me try?' he asked. When I nodded, he went on to say that he couldn't do the banister but, if I would settle for winders instead of a platform, he just might . . . he just might get the treads in.

I couldn't speak. All I could do was nod. Driving slowly back to the farm, I could barely see. Once in the front door, I let one sob escape and that was it. The dam burst. I couldn't stop. Half of me was howling and yowling and the other, sensible half was slapping on cold water and briskly ordering me to stop that noise. I seemed to be two people. While all this was going on, a third party joined us. Anxious little feet were padding alongside, running circles around my feet in the bathroom. They followed me into the sitting-room where I threw my sodden self onto the couch. Immediately Miranda was on my chest and shoving her furry little face up against mine. Her engine shifted into low gear, giving a reasonable imitation of a gravel truck on a steep grade. Nothing could prevail against it, and gradually we were breathing in unison, long and slow. When Gordon found us, the purrs had subsided into a long, gentle hum and I just had the hiccups. The builder was given his walking papers the next day.

It was three days before I had the strength to return to the house. As I held the handle of the front door, I could hear the tap of George's hammer and singing. George was singing? I opened the door and there were the stairs! Wonder of wonders! George, now looking anxious, explained that the risers were just a little higher than they should be and the treads shallower but that the three winders, triangular steps that complete the ninety-degree turn, were generous and safe.

'And you can't do the banister?'

'Nope. But I know who can. All we have to do is get him here before hayin' time.'

The oak newel posts, the handrails, and the turned balusters came from the stair people. Then I was elected go-between by the man who was telling me how to install it and George's friend who was doing the installation. Each accused the other of having an accent that couldn't be understood. Fortunately, they both had infinite patience, which waxed into enthusiasm. At one point, Fritz said to me over the phone, 'But this is wahnderful! Now you will alwiss know how to build a staircase.'

'But Fritz, I don't *want* to know.'

When George heard that the builder had gone, never to return, his joy was unconfined. He expressed it simply: 'That nut.'

We felt we were not too bright ourselves, but when we appealed to the architect he assured us that he was then working with two builders who were even worse. 'Yours was no good, I'll admit, but he was better.' He had really good builders, of course, and I knew of several more by then. They were all booked solid for the next two years.

Then the calls came in. The first caller was razing his half-built house back to the concrete block and starting again. Did we know of a good builder? Another was completing his 'can of worms', selling for what he could get, and starting again somewhere else. Did we know a good builder? Another had taken over and was doing it all with his own two hands. Did we know a good plumber? We found this cheering. We had company. The world was full of nuts.

'George. Do you know of a good builder?'

'Now, wait a minute. Let's take a tour of the house. At first, I figured it was none of my business. Now I figure it is.'

At the end of the tour, I thought what I needed was a demolition crew, but then I remembered the house of the tired garden. We had ripped out wires and plumbing and refloored. The workmen had been first class. I knew the man who would take out the insides of the fireplaces and rebuild them and the man who would sand our floors back to the raw wood and begin again. We had started out to build a house that would look like an old house rebuilt. Now we were going to have a new house that would be rebuilt to look like an old house rebuilt.

'See?' said George. 'I knew you could do it.' The question was, would *they* do it? How would I reach them?

There was a phone at the farm, which we shared on a party line with Elsie—with Elsie and her sister. They both had shack fever. When the deep snow comes to this part of the world, many of the ladies find themselves marooned inside their houses once their husbands have gone off to work in the only car. This solitary confinement leads to shack fever, and the only way to alleviate it is to get on the phone and talk all day. Elsie was really very nice. I could have the phone to call out at any time, but anyone trying to return my call would get nothing but a busy signal. The thing to do was get the phone installed at the house and move in. Ready or not, we had to move in.

Water Water Everywhere

The first spring thaw came in late February, with the sun rapidly melting the five-foot drifts beside the roads. Since the frost was still in the ground, all this water roiled the surface into mud. Not too bad at first—not too bad until the skies opened up and it rained on and on and on. This really took the frost out of the soil and, with cars barely able to toil their way through the mud, we were all longing for the days when there was nothing to contend with but snow, freezing rain, and fog.

George and the heater, their work completed, had now departed, so Gordon left the farm early every morning to give the house a quick inspection. All was well for the first few days and then he heard a dripping noise; water was coming through one of the bedroom ceilings. He climbed into the attic and was so intent on gazing up at the roof that he performed a Rumpelstiltskin and put his foot down through the plaster. When he reported this, he ordered me to keep cool, stay put and don't worry.

Elsie released the phone over to me and a quick go-through of every roofer in the district disclosed the fact that they had all gone to Florida, all of them to a man. Nancy C. had lived in the district for years and would be sure to know of someone who could nail a shingle on a roof, so I called her. Half-way through my explanation she said, 'Be right there,' and hung up.

'No, Nancy! No!' I was talking to the air. At first I didn't know where 'there' was, the farm or the house. Then I decided it had to be the house and slithered off in the car; but it was too late. I could see the farm truck at the foot of our drive and her foreman Ed standing on the hill, and Nancy was marching with great determination up the drive itself. With the thaw a spring had risen at the top and centre of the drive and undermined the entire slope, turning it into a quagmire.

I called, shouted, waved, and the wind blew my words back into my face. She couldn't hear, but Ed saw my semaphore signals and ran after her. Just as she sank well over the top of her rubber boots, he popped her out and deposited her on dry ground. Then he went back to retrieve the boots.

While Ed nailed plywood onto the roof, Nancy and I sat in the kitchen, drying her feet with old rags. I had to explain that we had no water. You may recall that the first thing, the very first thing, you do in the country is sink the well, *before* you build. We knew that and we did that. They went down two hundred feet, installed an immense pump, and assured us that we had five gallons a minute. Then Hydro went on strike so we couldn't turn on the pump. However, Hydro was now back in business, and when the pump came on we discovered we had five gallons a minute of purple mud and hastily turned it off again. The three fireplaces had been rebuilt and the floors refinished, but there was no water in the faucets or the heating pipes; no heat, no water, bare wood, bare plaster, and a hole in the roof.

'You are not moving in,' said Nancy.

'If we're ever to get hold of all this, I have to have a two-way phone,' said I, and explained about Elsie.

'You can *not* live here.' She looked very worried, then broke into a bright smile. 'You really can't. The mover can't get up the driveway.'

Our landlord had all the same things to say. He had called in to advise and console: 'Now just relax. Take it easy. If you can't get out, the new tenants can't get in here. They know that.' He glanced out at the road and said, 'You'd never get a loaded van along that without a bulldozer.'

I flew out to the hall and grabbed the phone. 'Elsie! I need the line.'

Most of our furniture was in storage with the local movers, who had been promising to build an ark. Now when I said, 'Bulldozer?' they were game. Why not? They were weary of sitting in the office watching the rain. In three days it was dry overhead and six strong young men in rubber boots arrived at the farm with one van loaded, another empty for the contents of the farm, and two large bulldozers.

'Got it all worked out,' they said. Two boys in socks worked inside and handed everything out the door to the boys in boots. Around about noon we upped anchor and tacked east, beating up to windward. The heavy machines squeezed the mud flat so that Miranda and I could follow in the car.

'You're going to your new house,' I told her and she let out a wail of anguish and despair.

'Listen, it beats the barn,' I said, but as we skidded from side to side along the road, I wondered about that. No heat. No water. We had three fireplaces but no firewood. Gordon was going to carry water in, in plastic containers.

People came to their doors to watch as our cavalcade made its ponderous way and at last we were at the foot of our gelatine hill. Here the bulldozers dug in and dragged the vans axle-deep up the hill to the front door where they slowly sank to a stop. Now the boys put the former procedure into reverse and I began to learn something about the local character. The tougher it is, the better they like it. When, at long last, they towed the vans away, every piece of furniture was exactly where it should be. Miranda's basket was set neatly beside the empty fireplace. They'd done everything but make the beds, and not one drop of mud was inside the house.

That night, Gordon brought up an arm-load of wood from the basement and set it up in the fireplace. Once alight it drew well, and the warmth came out into the room. Miranda found a down cushion, rolled over onto her back and turned into the most beautiful cat in the world.

'That, ladies, is the most expensive fire you'll ever sit beside.'

'What is it?'

'The door trim, window trim and baseboards. It's like burning five-dollar bills.' He looked remarkably cheerful. We were all cheerful. We were home.

Once the roads were passable, my tile man, my plumber and my electrician arrived and set to work, ripping out and reinstalling, and, out of deference to my presence, keeping their anger and disgust down to a low grumble and mumble. Then the roofer arrived from Toronto. He bade me a bright good morning and climbed the ladder. I left him to his inspection. He was up there all alone under the empty sky, for miles around not a soul was to be seen, and after some tramping back and forth he let it all out. Completely unaware that his voice was thundering down all three chimneys, amplified and reverberating, he gave out with the most magnificent oratorio in plain and fancy swearing that I have ever heard. You could have set it to Wagner: it said what we all felt, blew the windows open and cleared the air. After that, we all felt better. The house felt better. People who cared were now in charge. And I gathered we were going to have a new roof.

A Drop to Drink

Just to prove that the situation was well in hand and everything coming back to normal, we accepted an invitation to the Hunt Ball. Black tie. Though attending this soirée might present a few problems, none of them surely would be insurmountable. The first problem was how to make our way from the house to the car through knee-high weeds over the ridge and down the slippery Winter Road, so named because it is used in bad weather. Gordon decided he could wrap his trousers tight round his shins and get them down into his rubber boots. I had chosen a long jersey dress for the occasion. With a little experimentation, I discovered that the skirt could be hoicked up to the waist and then twisted in front in much the manner one wrings out a towel, and then thrown over the shoulder; the whole to be anchored by my coat. I just had to hope no one would help me off with the coat at the front door. To this ensemble I added the inevitable rubber boots. Dot, my immediate neighbour, had suggested that her husband ride us out on his old, high, and swaying tractor—she and Harold had attended their first country dance on the same tractor—but we felt we could cope.

The real problem was to take a shower. We had that magnificent shower stall with a drain that worked. If you're interested, it can be done. Heating water in the electric kettle, we filled a plastic pail. A floor sponge took care of the soaping part, then the whole pail of clear water was sluiced down from the neck. Still a little soapy, we donned our best bib and tucker and went to the ball. It was marvellous. We met old friends and made new; danced, drank, ate and talked. So why, on our return, was I suddenly struck down with a *crise de nerfs*?

It may have been the hour: three o'clock in the morning. It may have been the place: I was standing on top of the ridge, clutching two plastic jugs of water. It may have been the mice:

thousands of them were skittering and squealing in all directions, running over the toes of my boots. Trying to fight it down, I raised my face to the black velvet sky, alive with stars, gazed out at the lights of Toronto winking on the horizon, and thought of the beautiful five hundred thousand acres in between. But doubt—or was it sanity—struck.

'What in the name of God am I doing here? At three in the morning?'

Gordon came up over the ridge with the flashlight and two more jugs of water. As no reply had descended from the stars, I asked Gordon. 'What are we *doing* here?'

Ever unflappable, he said we were carrying in the water and going to bed.

So it's always darkest before the dawn, and with the dawn came the sun. Suddenly the frost was out of the subsoil. The land was at last draining straight down through as well as over the top, and Jon came over the ridge and into the kitchen.

Jon believes in leaving us all to our own devices until we get into trouble, when he will arrive mysteriously and quietly take over. He has been doing this since he could stand up, and one way or another we have given him a lot of practice. We were overjoyed to see him, not because we thought we were in trouble, but because we wanted to try out a few new ideas. Peering through the windows, we could see which way the surface water was running and now knew which way to grade. As we sat over coffee, we wanted to know what he thought of using four-inch perforated PVC pipe, running it down from the far corner of the garage and out over the hill. Should we lay it on gravel? Should we bury it?

Jon regarded us steadily.

'There is no water in the house.'

'Yes, dear, we know. But there's lots outside.' No laugh.

Gordon said, 'The PVC pipe won't be enough. We should regrade the driveway so that it leads away from the garage and out over the bank.'

Jon pointed firmly to the kitchen faucet.

'We'll get to that,' said Gordon.

'No, Dad. Now. Water,' said Jon. He wasn't letting go. Nothing would divert him.

Well, it seemed that Gordon knew a man who had a friend who knew a man who had had his well fixed by another very good man. With Jon nipping at our heels the phone calls went through, and before I could perc another pot of coffee, the very good man was sitting with us in the kitchen. He was the most silent man I had ever met.

'Would screens work?' Negative shake of his head.

'Should we dig another well?' He took a sip of coffee.

We gave him a full description of the old well, two hundred feet deep, the type of pump. He looked at the far wall. But when Gordon went with him out the door, he became positively loquacious. 'I'll call back. Have to talk to Dad.'

None of this seemed any too hopeful to me, but Jon reassured us. 'He was thinking. He'll be back and he'll fix it. Now let's talk about the PVC pipe.'

He came back and he fixed it. He raised the pump up fifty feet out of the mud, slowed it down so that it stopped behaving like an egg-beater, and led the water into a thousand-gallon settling tank, which filled up overnight. We had a thousand gallons a day. When I turned on the faucet, clear water flowed. When I turned on the HOT faucet, HOT water came out. When we ran it into the radiators, we had heat. Who invented American plumbing? Why don't we run up a memorial to him? In every town and city, a statue of him in the main square. Let me be the first to subscribe.

Our well man is as talkative as ever. Ten years later, I phoned to ask if we could dispense with the holding tank.

'Working?'

'Oh, yes.'

'Don't touch it.'

You know where you are with a man like that.

So we had a house, a well, and no driveway. In the last rain, the entire slope, fifty feet long and two feet deep, had slid to the bottom. The time had come to rebuild and, if there was one thing I did know, it was how to build a road. My father built roads. He should have had a dozen boys but all he had was me, and when I was eight he decided to make my acquaintance. On Sundays, he would drive me out to the job and, while he was looking it over, he would explain clearly and in detail how a road was built.

First the road bed was dug out to firm ground, then eight inches of four-inch rock added, followed by finer and finer gravel packed firm. On this deep and monumental bed you then laid, not asphalt, but Warrenite Bitulithic. Then you stamped in a brass plate on which these words were engraved. That was a *good* road. He once took me for a walk down the Roman Road near Chester in England. We jumped up and down on it. It had been there two thousand years. That, he said, was a *real* road.

I grew up wanting to build roads, but when I was sixteen he talked me out of it, as it had now become apparent that I was a girl. The ambition had never died and now, when I walked out to that driveway, I could see my chance. I was going to build a road with a good, firm base, eight inches of four-inch rock, and settle for asphalt.

Two gentlemen came from the local paving firm and I explained what I wanted, leaving out only the brass plate. One of them stared dumbfounded and the other subsided onto a convenient rock. 'Oh,' he said, 'Oh, how I'd love to build a road like that! Lady, have you any idea what it would cost? Just the hill alone? Golly!' We parted filled with mutual respect.

I knew surface grading wouldn't fix that hill, and while I was still waiting for inspiration to strike, Bruce arrived. Bruce is a big, confident man. Word had got around, he said, that I wanted to fix the drive. And he could beat anybody's price.

'Wait 'til you hear what I want,' I said. 'They didn't even give me a price.' He heard me out and didn't bat an eye; just invited me to come out and look at the job. First, the spring. It was going to rise, right there, every March, so the thing to do was lead it off with perforated pipe into the ditch and down the hill and let it empty into the gully at the bottom. Just to make sure, we'd bury PVC pipe down both ditches. Shades of Roy E. Biles! There's a section drawing in *Garden Magic* showing you that this is what you do with a bothersome spring. While he had me faint with admiration, Bruce asked me if I'd settle for four inches of four-inch rock. 'We'll dig down to a firm base first.'

'Are you just going to load the trucks, open up the back, and let it roll out?'

'We're not going to lay it by hand.'

'How many loads?'

'Four.'

'How about five?'

'OK.'

'And the fine gravel?'

He pointed to the small mountain at the foot of the hill. 'There it is. And that's your surface material. If you pave this hill, you'll never get up it when the ice is on it.'

The price was right and the road was right. I'm proud of that hill road and so is Bruce. I was prouder still when he called by one day and said, 'A friend of yours wants me to put in his drive. How would you like to come round and show me what he wants?' That was a great day. I had everything but a hard hat.

III

The Country Garden

*"Keep safely and warily
thine uttermost fence"*
— THOMAS TUSSER,
Hundreth Pointes of Good Husbandrie (1557)

It Grows Beautiful Weeds

On the twenty-fourth of May people in this climate, if they are cautious, finally bring their plants out of the greenhouse, open their packets of seeds and set them in the good earth. On our first twenty-fourth of May, it was all too apparent that we had no good earth in which to set anything. I had ordered a small load of cow manure and a small load of topsoil, which had been dumped at the front of the circle contained by the driveway. Anxious friends had brought me cuttings and Mary had contributed the mock orange that was crowding her driveway. This we had dug out with a large root-ball in which strange little green things were growing. As there was no place to put them, we simply heeled them into the pile of topsoil.

The land still lay bare. Fine dust blew about where it had been scarified by the bulldozer, and the circle was still undisturbed cow pasture. Only now did I begin to realize where we were and what we had. We were on the top of the Niagara Escarpment in Dufferin County. Our property had been bought as Crown land in the early 1800s by the McBrides and hadn't been plowed since the glaciers had harrowed the ground, leaving great granite stones behind them. Mr. McBride had cleared out trees where our house now stood and planted fruit trees, which were destroyed by a blizzard. But he hadn't plowed. Much, much later, local farmers had turned their cows loose on our hills to eat the wild grasses, and, while they were at it, they had chewed down the young shoots coming from old apple-tree roots. By the time we came, the cows had been long gone and young trees were shooting up about six feet high from the old roots. A neighbour said there had never been an orchard here and they were wild apples. Then why were they precisely twenty feet apart and set in the classic contour pattern to be used on hills? We cleared out a few shoots and left them alone.

No time to worry about apples. The real problem was the earth or lack of it. It wasn't just that I couldn't get a spade into it. No one could. No one ever had.

Nancy C. said, 'What you need is a plan. Then each year do one part of it. And face the facts. You can't do it yourself.'

I called Walter. I had tried to tell him the problems, but all he had heard was 'a house in the country'. He came roaring up in his truck, all smiles, but when he got out of the truck, his face fell.

'Why did you build this tall house here? It is sticking up like a chimney. It should be cradled with trees!' His hands waved, planting a veritable forest of trees.

I told him about the need for a plan, something to make house and land more compatible. He nodded and began a tour, striding about, growing less and less buoyant, and at last picked up a handful of the ground. 'What is this stuff?'

'It's like pit-run, Walter, what they use to surface the roads—it packs down hard.'

He let it drizzle out of his hand. I had never expected to see a look of despair on his face, but there it was. 'How can we grow anything in this?'

'It grows beautiful weeds.'

He stopped short and stared at me, then decided to ignore such nonsense. 'I don't know. I am going to have to think about this.' He drove away and I thought at the time he might never come back, but I *should* have known.

He came back and brought with him the strangest assortment of tools and machinery I had ever seen. There were wooden rakes with long tines set about four inches apart and he set his team to work with these, pulling off rocks the size of baseballs and only lightly scratching the surface.

'You're not going to till it?'

'Golly no. We'll just get more rocks.'

While that was going on, Walter brought forward what I think was a tractor. On the back of it was an immense paddle wheel, big enough to drive a show-boat down the Mississippi.

'There may be some good stuff over here,' he called. He stationed his contraption over by the cedar-rail fence and set the great wheel flying while the tractor stood still. Turf, rocks and dirt flew in all directions with the wheel reaching down deep. When he'd worked up a patch about twenty by twenty, he said, 'That's your vegetable garden.' Then the tractor was brought up beside the kitchen door. Here the plasterers, carpenters and stucco men had dumped everything, including their lunch bags. Again the wheel churned until all the area up to the foot of the ridge and the full length of the house was loose. It was appalling stuff, but it was loose.

Now, while his men went to work with their rakes on what were to be the vegetable garden and the side garden, Walter slung a big canvas bag over one shoulder, filled it with pasture mix, and went striding over the bare ground, flinging out seed in great arcs as he walked and looking strangely biblical.

'I used to do this when I was a lad,' he called.

When I went over to look, he told me that there was a lot of good clover in it, which puts nitrogen into the ground.

'Will it bring back the wildflowers?'

'Who knows?' He looked out over the bare earth and then his familiar look of confidence returned. I still hold fast to what he said then.

'The land heals itself.'

At the end of the day, I stood by the truck as Walter prepared to drive off and gave me my last instructions. 'You play around with that for awhile and see what happens. Let me know. See over there? I've left you some of my own good topsoil.' The truck started to move away and then he couldn't help himself. He popped his head back out the window and called, 'It grows byootiful weeds!'

Taking heart, I bought an assortment of vegetable seeds and Gene brought me tomato plants. It was now June, a little late to be planting and, as well, the ground was too lumpy to be raked. I pounded it with a mattock, put the seeds in and hoped for the best.

Gordon came up with the idea for the side garden. Use the leftover chimney bricks to design a parterre; cover the paths with gravel and use some of Walter's beautiful topsoil to fill the beds. But what to plant in the parterre? The beds had only a top-dressing of good soil, so it couldn't be anything that sent down deep roots. Herbs. I looked up herbs. Herbs like a poor soil. If that's what they liked that was what they were going to get, and wouldn't it all look charming with little green mats growing in the circles and triangles?

Did you know that dill grows five feet high, that sage and hyssop turn into three-foot woody shrubs? Nothing was less than a foot, even the basil and lemon balm. The thyme replanted itself in the gravel paths. I had a herb garden but couldn't find the parterre. Canterbury bells and borage frothed along the wall of the house, humming with bees. The vegetables grew and the clover came up lush and green. It was chaotic but thriving in 'this stuff'.

I still wanted a plan.

The hills rolled off in every direction of the compass, not a straight line anywhere, and paths were appearing where we walked to the woods or to the top of the long ridge. I couldn't think where to begin. Help arrived in the form of Jon, Liz and David. Each went about it in his own way. Jon said to plant the circle enclosed by the driveway to grass. 'Then, where the topsoil's been dumped along the front of it, you can have a real flower border. Plants are growing in it now.' When I went out to have a look, I found the funny little green things that had come riding in with the mock orange were now unmistakably phlox and delphinium.

Liz set herself to the task that was obviously waiting to be done and weeded the parterre and the vegetable garden. 'Never mind. It's all going to be beautiful. You'll see.' Her faith would move mountains and inspired me to gather bushel baskets of the mustard weed the 'dozer had stirred up.

David, who believes that the taking or giving of advice is a monumental waste of time, simply took a pick and shovel to dig great holes and helped us manhandle the mock orange into them. After that, he sent me a copy of *Findhorn Garden*. The message, none too subtle, was that only a miracle could save me now. He had seen all too clearly what lay below the surface: a gravel pit.

We all thought the grass circle was a good idea, but how to get it in?

A strange little magazine kept turning up once a month in our rural mail-box. It was a chock-a-block with the most extraordinary ideas, some of them hilarious, I thought. It was called *Organic Gardening*. One evening I sat leafing through this while Gordon read the paper and Jon read a book. A picture caught my eye. A determined elderly woman was standing beside a large red tiller and behind them both was a luxuriant green market garden.

'Gordon, there's a picture here of a tiller.'

No reply.

'The woman who uses it is eighty. Her name is Mame.'

He didn't even rustle his paper.

'I'm only sixty-two.'

Silence.

'If she can use it, I can use it. It tills up hard turf.'

'What?' Jon was up and sitting beside me. 'Let's see that.' He read it all carefully, then moved over beside his Dad and started talking about bolo tines in the rear, precision gears, electric start and one-hand control. Man talk.

The Troy arrived in the last week of June. It was a little late to be putting in a lawn, but the tiller was there and we had to try it. At first we kept both hands on it, then one hand, then no hands. The area was flat and the machine rolled along turning up rocks, a few Coke bottles and more rock. When we finished, we had an indescribable mess of rocks.

'We'll have to get that off before we till again.'

I went looking for one of Walter's stone rakes, but no one had ever heard of them. In the end, we bought a rake with long tines and cut out every other one. It worked, but it wasn't easy.

We spread manure and tilled again: more rock and more raking. At this point I was all for spreading the grass seed, but Jon—and I still can't believe this—harnessed himself and his father to heavy boards with ropes and the pair of them dragged these back and forth until they were satisfied that it was level. If you're wondering why we didn't hire someone else to do all this, all I ask is, who else would be that crazy?

The seed was spread and watered and lo, a fine green whisker appeared. The topsoil was spread around the front of the circle and the phlox and delphiniums placed with the few annuals that could be found so late in the season.

We didn't have a garden, but the bare ground was gone, the pasture mix was lush, and now we knew a garden was possible. I called Walter with the glorious news. 'Plants will grow here!' He said he would come to us first the following spring, with a PLAN.

Someone once told me that you should never decorate a house until you've lived in it. 'Give the house time to tell you what it wants,' she said. I began to wonder if that would work with a garden. And I didn't have to wonder for long. Late July and August came with burning blue sky, hot winds and endless, endless sun. The garden didn't *tell* me—it shouted for shade and screamed for water; the plants were shrivelling in the heat and so were we. We were spending the summer out in the country and living inside. We couldn't wait for a plan. We ordered six mature trees and a swimming pool.

Pests in the Garden

This chapter is usually the last in garden books. I don't know why. The theory may be that it is too off-putting or that the pests don't arrive until the garden is in. But here I am attempting to tell the unvarnished truth, and the truth about a country garden is that all the pests are in residence before you set foot on the place. They are the original inhabitants and they will not be moved.

Innocent of all this, I was making a futile attempt on a lovely summer morning to sleep in late, clinging to my pillow as to a life-raft. But the sun was up streaming in the window, birds were up and singing their heads off. There was just too much noise going on, and at length I lured myself up and out with the thought of a lovely hot cup of coffee, to be sipped out in the garden, gazing at the view. After a quick shower, I walked briskly into the kitchen, picked up a kettle and went to the sink to fill it. I was face to face with a large bull.

He was on the outside of the window looking in. I was on the inside looking out. For a bull, he appeared to be quite affable, with his little tufty wig between his horns, standing knee-deep in the borage and Canterbury bells. For the moment he was mesmerized by the water flowing from the faucet. Before I could realize that I really was seeing what I was seeing, a great uproar broke out at the front of the house and, abandoning the bull, I ran to the front windows. There, gambolling fetlock-deep in the new lawn, were all his wives and children. One small calf had discovered that if he ran over the top of a small evergreen it tickled his tummy, so he would swing round and charge over it again. The rest just milled about and most found the clover on the far side of the drive.

I hadn't met the owners, but I knew who they were and phoned. In minutes I saw a diminutive blonde coming up the driveway. When I peered timidly out the door, she called, 'I'm Barbara. Come on, grab a rake!'

I went out and grabbed a rake, glancing nervously about. Where was that bull?

He appeared from the side of the house and Barbara fetched him a hearty whack on the rump. 'Move it,' she said to the bull and, to me, 'Don't mind him. He's a cream puff. Get going, Cecil!'

Unperturbed, Cecil moved off majestically down the drive. We ran about persuading the cows and calves to follow, Barbara still heartily whacking rumps. I dithered about but still had the rake perched confidently on one shoulder. At last the whole herd was in motion, Barbara still calling, 'Move it, move it.'

Puffs of dust rose around their hooves, the wine of the morning air was exhilarating, a cry was rising to my lips—'Head 'em up! Move 'em out!'—but before I was completely carried away, Barbara was shouting from the head of the line, 'Move 'em back!'

My God, were we all coming back to my place?

Fortunately, no. My presence was required at the front to help turn Cecil, who had decided to lead us all out to the highway. With some ado, we turned the herd into an apple orchard and, once out of that, they had to be jockeyed past another herd who had dashed to the fence to call affectionate greetings to Cecil. At last we were all milling about Barbara's gate. A man from up the road had come to assist but was useless, staggering about laughing and clinging to fence posts. We were saved at last by an old collie, who strolled out of Barbara's gate, gave us all a look of infinite contempt, and herded the whole shebang into their own yard. Barbara locked the gate. I don't know what I expected her to say, but it wasn't, 'Here we go again!'

'Again?'

'The fence is down. They'll just go around and out again. Can you drive a nail?'

The afternoon was spent repairing barbed-wire fence in company with Barbara and Dot, our immediate neighbour. She, foolish girl, had stopped to enquire what was happening, and before she knew it she was part of the work crew. I learned a lot. You don't plant clover near a herd of cows. The absolutely first requirement for a country garden is a fence, or you'll have bulls in the borage and cows in the clover.

Keep the fence in good repair; add a pair of stout gates, kept locked. If you can construct these so as to keep out dogs, you should. No fence will keep out deer, groundhogs, raccoons, porcupines, rabbits or skunks.

Groundhogs were the next problem (you may call them woodchucks). We had several, all of different personalities. One ate the outside telephone. 'All of it, Madame?' the operator enquired when I reported it. Well no, just the cord and anything plastic left outdoors. The others ate the vegetables, wiping out a complete planting at one go. We lined the fence with chicken-wire and they ate through it. We lined the fence with farmer's steel fencing and they climbed over or under. Their fur is so thick they don't feel, or don't mind, electric shocks. We bought a gun and they fell over laughing. Then we found the answer. A radio. At first it was tuned to music and they liked that. Then Gordon tuned it to a twenty-four-hour broadcast that gave the news, the weather, the stock-market report and the news, the weather, the stock-market report, on and on without cease. All the groundhogs left, bored right out of their minds. Because batteries wear out too soon, we ran a power line into the garden, then perched the radio on a platform up out of the wet. It had to have a cover to keep out the rain and keep off the sun, or the transistors would pop. But it worked! The deer still come onto the property and stroll about eating apple falls, but they avoid the vegetable garden with the radio going.

Here, if I may digress, a note on groundhogs. Groundhogs are supposed to have a life of only one year, but I know that the resident of the vegetable garden survived on and on. He grew to the size of a bear cub. He became friendly and would sit up on his haunches two rows behind where I was working. He developed a taste for beefeater tomatoes. The spring I noticed he was turning grey was rather depressing. 'Grow old along with me, the best is yet to be' I had always thought a charming sentiment—but no one had told me my companion would be a groundhog. When he was driven out by the stock-market report I felt unkind, forcing him to leave his home in the sere and yellow leaf.

Though the raccoons left us alone once I stopped growing corn, they came back for one glorious festive night. Tiny hard-backed beetles were inundating the raspberries and, having read that they would drown themselves in beer, I had hung cans of the stuff through the bushes. It was the raccoons who drowned themselves. They loved it and held a night-long riot-ous party. I don't know what you do about the beetles.

Skunks: Keep your distance. If you have adventurous pets, you can keep large tins of tomato juice on hand to remove the odour, but this is extremely messy, and I have been told vinegar works as well.

Rabbits: Rabbits had girdled and killed four large new maples before we found the answer to them. The snow falls so deep that they can stand above wire or plastic wrapping. Now we use SKOOT. It is made in Brampton, Ontario, and has saved us thousands in protecting every tree and shrub on the place. It doesn't gum up the sprayer as some products do, and one spraying in the fall lasts right through to the following November. It has the further advantage of allowing you to spray every twig and branch as high as you like.

Porcupines: SKOOT was no help here because they are not fur-bearing animals. It took us a while to discover that it was a porcupine who was eating the top three or four feet of the pine trees, and even longer to discover that this was also the culprit who was nipping off phlox and delphinium about six inches above the ground. (It doesn't eat these—just nips them off.) Then I used Benomyl to spray the phlox for mildew, and that turned out to be the cure. Benomyl is a systemic poison, and somehow the porcupines must be aware of it. It is, by the way, the only poison we use and we wear a mask when we do, also gloves. The porcupine who ate the bar stools and started on the walls of the pool cabana was captured in a Have-a-Heart trap.

Bait it with a sprinkling of ordinary table salt. What you do after that is up to you.

We have other assorted four-footed creatures who think they own the place—foxes, squirrels—and all you do here is make sure your pets get their rabies shots, which, by the way, doesn't protect you.

Insects

The next things on the agenda were the caterpillars and insects. You name it and we have it, so I shall deal with only those we have managed to control.

Tent caterpillars were festooned in deep webs in every tree on the property when we came here, not to mention all the trees along the roadside. I went down to the farmer's supply to see what was on offer, and as I shopped along the shelves, reading labels, I was stopped short by the magic words *Bacillus thuringiensis* (Bt.). Merlin! The customs had let it through! I nearly phoned to tell him. I bought it for us. I bought it for the neighbours. We sprayed every nest we could find. And the result proved to be nearly total victory. Last year I found only two small nests. However, we still use it for caterpillars of all types, particularly that little green fellow who lets himself down on a fine thread from the maple trees, the same one we met in the Tired Garden.

A similar green caterpillar appeared on the columbine, leaving the bloom but demolishing all the leaves. Bt. had a strange effect on these: each generation was half the size of the former until we were down to little green dots. But then I tried rotenone, with complete success. Now I sprinkle rotenone on all the columbines when the leaves are a fresh new green. It can be used on vegetables too, but I don't put anything on mine except the onion and garlic spray—I know we can eat onions and garlic. Tomato worms are cut off with the leaf, slipped under the mulch and stepped on. Marigolds are planted in the vegetable garden to control nematodes and because they look cheerful and pretty.

However, we came to deep trouble in the vegetable garden. Young Norman, our latest and most industrious helper, came flying down to the kitchen door, only having just gone up the hill to weed. His eyes were popping. 'The whole garden's moving. It's horrible.' I ran back with him, and indeed it was horrible. The entire sixty-by-forty-feet was thick with earwigs, a living, moving carpet of brown earwigs. (They look like half-inch cigars with two little antennae at the front and pincers at the rear, and appear to be hard-backed.) I sent Norman off to weed the ivy bank and sat down to think. There's always an answer. To every problem there's an answer. Earwigs like the dark and they like moisture, so they had been breeding like crazy under the mulch. Take the mulch off and expose them to the sun? Till them under? Ugh! Then I remembered an article in *Organic Gardening* about that stuff that scratches: ground-up sea-shells, Fossil Flower. When I read it to Gordon, he said, 'That's Diatomaceous Earth. There's a fifty-pound bag of it in the pool house. You buy it at the pool supply.'

I got the wheelbarrow and the fifty-pound bag and applied it by the shovelful, sweeping it over the whole garden with every throw until it looked like a light snow. The next day I went up to see if I could find a dead earwig. There were no dead earwigs, no live earwigs, no earwigs. Unbelieving, I dug down in the earth and still no earwigs. Eventually, I found the article and learned that D.E. is for soft-bodied insects, so either earwigs are soft-bodied or D.E. works on hard-backed as well. At any rate, it is effective. I sprinkled it around the doorways as well, and the creatures stopped coming in the house. We didn't abandon the mulch. First we take it off and sprinkle D.E. on the earth, then we reapply the mulch. This has worked ever since. But a word of caution: D.E. kills earthworms as well, so apply it early and sparingly—not, as I did, by the shovelful. 'Sparingly' is a good word to keep in mind. Don't try to kill everything in sight. The bugs fight back. Wouldn't you? The simple methods that encourage them to go and live someplace else work best.

Another mysterious disappearance took place with the roses.

They were thick with aphids. In desperation, I came off organic and used Black Leaf 40. It killed where it hit and more aphids came back. I remembered how garlic had driven them off before and went off to the market this time. They had no garlic in, or chives. Tentatively, the girl offered me a box of six leek plants. I'll try anything once, so I brought them home and planted them, and the same overnight miracle took place. I fondly think the leeks can't be seen in the rose beds, but they have received so many comments that I have to admit they can be seen, though I cut them back. Garlic chives look better. At any rate— no aphids. For black spot on the roses I used to alternate sprayings of Benomyl with another fungicide, as the fungus builds up resistance to each in turn. But now, in search of an organic substitute, I use Safer's Natural Fungicide or dust with D.E. As it is mechanical rather than chemical, there should be no resistance build-up in the fungus spores.

Wild or tame, apples were appearing on our apple trees, the buggiest apples you ever did see. At apple-picking time the game was to find an apple without a worm in it. On enquiry we learned that ten sprays a year were mandatory. For a while we thought we'd rather have wormy apples. However, we sprayed with dormant oil, which seemed to reduce the crop. Then we sprayed with Bt. It helped a little. Then we read about apple-tree traps and tried that. We bought bags of round red and round yellow plastic Christmas-tree ornaments, which had neat little loops on the top and came with their own twistems. These were thoroughly gooed up with Tanglefoot, a sticky substance sold for applying around the tree trunk. Right after blossom fall, we put about six of these sticky plastic 'apples' in each tree. That year we had an abundant crop of half wormy and half non-wormy fruit. The traps were thick with insects. They say it takes about three years to get a clean crop, which worries me. What are we going to do with all those apples?

In the spring, black flies and mosquitoes devour the gardener anxious to finish the early planting; my scalp gets so bumpy I'm ashamed to go to the hairdresser for fear they'll think I have a frightful disease. We use a lot of OFF and, better still, Muskol.

We were about to resort to the bug lights that zap them when the barn swallows came. Three of us reclined round the pool one evening discussing which bug light to buy, when a swallow flashed down and skimmed the pool. Soon there were twenty or more sieving the air round our heads, a delightful aerial display, and we forgot about lights.

Our bird feeders go up in November when the jays come to the back door and scold us. We take them down in the spring when the grackles arrive. The feeders and a mixed shrubbery keep birds with us all year.

Weeds

It may seem strange to list weeds under garden pests—but if they're not pests, what are they? I learned in time what Walter meant about his beautiful weeds. When you pull them out, they stay out. Our indigenous weeds are so full of fight that if you pull one, they call out the Marines; they send in the heavy artillery and come marching over the hill, underground and through the air, in battalions. We had thistles we had to cut down with an axe, and thirty more would pop up round the stem. Most of these thrived on top of that ridge among the stones and mice. And here I decided to move the vegetable garden. I know the good soil is at the bottom of a hill, but as we had no good soil, top or bottom, what difference could it make? It would be awkward to water, but it would be out of sight. I know too that a vegetable garden can be beautiful—I've seen the pictures: rows and rows of matching cabbages without a gap. Does no one eat them? I have yet to see it in real life. All I wanted was a food factory.

The tiller was turned loose on the ridge and we went through the same process as with the front lawn. Remove the rocks. Till again, adding manure, and remove the rocks. We had overdone it this time and fenced in sixty by forty feet. The vegetables grew but couldn't be seen for the wild carrot, thistles and plants I couldn't put a name to. A little weeding each day didn't make a dent.

When Gordon announced that he'd be leaving early and coming back late, I saw my chance. 'Now, take it easy,' he said as he left. I was in full fighting regalia and he had a suspicion. As his car turned out of the drive I whipped out the wheelbarrow, loaded it with the axe, mattock, hoe and rake, sprayed myself with OFF and charged up the hill. Weeds, here I come! It was 7:30 in the morning and by 7:30 that night I had dug, whacked, axed and forked over all but one row of carrots. I suppose it looked beautiful, but I couldn't see. I was covered with black-fly bites, dirt, and perspiration still pouring in rivers. The salt was stinging my eyes and every bone ached. I seem always to be addressing the heavens from the top of that ridge; this time I rocked back on my heels and said, 'Is this what I'm *supposed* to be doing? Really?'

A soft voice behind me said, 'Mrs. K. What *are* you doing?'

In the words of the old vaudevillian, slowly I turned, feeling somewhat prickly on the scalp, but it was just Ross, leaning on the fence. Ross is a young farmer who lives south of us. He looked so cool and fresh and clean and I knew what I looked like.

Trying to sound reasonably sane, I said, 'I'm just weeding these carrots.'

Still soft and easy, Ross smiled. 'You know, Mrs. K., I've met Mr. K. and he struck me as being a kind man, even generous.'

I nodded feebly.

'Well, I'll bet if you were nice to him—I mean really nice—I'll bet he'd buy you a bunch of carrots.'

Having delivered his punchline, Ross collected me from where I lay, escorted me firmly to the kitchen, and took two cold beers out of the fridge. Still kind and firm as a mother, he told me the facts of life about weeds. You don't pull them out: you slice them off at ground level or you smother them with mulch. You don't leave long grass growing right up to your house; it breeds black flies, mosquitoes and everything that stings and bites. You cut it down with a bush-hog.

'What's a bush-hog?' I was only faintly interested.

'You'll find out in the morning.' Ross wished me a good night and I took myself off to a hot bath and bed. I was so glad I'd insisted on a bath I could lie down in.

A bush-hog is a huge rotary mower attached to the back of a tractor. In the hands of a poor operator it can tear the ground to pieces, but Ross set it high, drove it easy, and cut back two hundred feet all around the house. It looked nice. He left the trout lily where it grew in a long wide band by the cedar-rail fence. He went round the wild asparagus we didn't know we had and left it on its own island. And he showed me where to cut back shrubs and let the trilliums out into the light where they could thrive. Late that night he came back with bales of hay and stacked them by the vegetable garden to be used as mulch.

I learned in time to use not only hay but stone, bark chips and grass cuttings for mulch. They all have different uses. I learned, too, to use a scuffle hoe to cut weeds off at the ankles. (Rain enters the stem and rots them.) I'm not fond of peat moss as mulch: it cakes and takes away too much moisture from the plants.

So there you have it. On our medicinal shelf you will find a fence, a gate, mulch, *Bacillus thuringiensis*, rotenone, SKOOT, onion and garlic spray, leeks, marigolds, Diatomaceous Earth, Tanglefoot, one Have-a-Heart trap, birds, coffee (for ants—see p. 27) and the only poison: Benomyl. Oh, and a magazine called *Organic Gardening*. I like to use things I'm not afraid of, but the real reason I garden organic is that it is the effective and permanent solution. The chemicals are temporary.

Make Your Own

The following tale is ten years compressed. Looking back, it took us longer than Neanderthal Man to learn how to garden, and all the time the answer was sitting in our pockets like the winning lottery ticket. We just didn't know it was there. The garden was telling us what it wanted and we couldn't hear. Each problem was tackled as it arose, which gave us no time to think.

Ross had so simplified our battle of the bugs and weeds that I was now inclined to ask advice of any farmer and so posed a question to an old boy who was repairing the fence. The reply was not immediate. He cogitated. Then he shifted weight from one foot to the other. 'Well, I'll tell yuh.' He removed the hat, scratched his head, replaced the hat. 'It's like this.' I now received a piercing glance from under the brim. 'It don't matter whut y'do, whut y'll git is aggravation.'

As time went on, I had thoughts of having this pronouncement cut in stone and set up as a sun dial in the herb garden.

The front lawn had been tilled down and reseeded after the visit of Cecil and the cows but, with little rain, the germination had been poor, more weeds than grass, so we tilled down and planted more grass. The following spring, this was so spotty that we tilled it down again and ordered grass sod. The men who laid the sod said, 'Nice topsoil,' and I said, 'That's not topsoil, it's our old lawn.'

The mulch Ross had brought was spread on the vegetable garden. Some of the bales were greener than others and I wanted it fluffy and golden like the magazine pictures, so the green bales were spread first and the golden bales put on top. Very pretty, but the vegetables were still too small to show. In less than a week the golden colour turned to green. In a very short time it was greener still, and, after a good rain, it was tall, lush green. I called Ross who came up the hill, took one look and said, 'Oh my golly. It's a field of oats.' He had pulled the bales out in the dark of the barn, delivered them in the dark and not noticed the four green bales. He tried not to laugh, looked contrite, thought we could pull it out. But in the end I tilled it all down, all of it, oats, hay, vegetables, and set myself to plant again. While I was doing that, the man who was landscaping the swimming pool came up to ask me a question and stopped short, looked in amazement and said, 'Topsoil? On top of the hill? There's none down there.'

I said, 'It's not topsoil. It's my old vegetable garden.'

Whenever anyone worked around the place lifting turf, collecting weeds, raking leaves, cutting grass, the constant question was, 'Where do you want this stuff?' I kept waving a vague arm to the top of the hill and saying, 'Behind the vegetable garden, where it's out of sight.' I assumed they would spread it out but soon discovered they were stacking it into an immense mound that couldn't be moved by hand. Each year it grew and when I couldn't bear the sight of it any longer, I asked Doug, who was grading the road into the woods, if his baby grader could handle it. When I went up to see how he was making out, he was sitting still on the grader grinning down at a nicely graded patch, fifty by fifty feet. 'Know what this is?' I didn't. 'Topsoil. Two feet deep right where I'm sitting.' I was so delighted, I planted it to asparagus and raspberries.

Now if it had all happened that fast and with that precision I might not have been so obtuse. Fate decided to give me a smart rap on the skull to sharpen my wits.

I wanted to enlarge the perennial border and plant shrubs on the steep side ridge, too steep to take the tiller. Walter said we'd dig big holes and fill them with topsoil and peat moss. He would bring the peat moss and I would order the topsoil. I had had several bad experiences with purchased topsoil. One lot had been dark and moist but had dried out and shown itself to be pulverized bark. Another lot was sand. When this lot arrived, I asked the driver not to unload it until I had looked at it.

'You going to climb up there?'

Without a fifteen-foot ladder I couldn't climb up there. He opened the back of the huge truck and rolled it all out; it was very dark and very gritty. When Walter arrived, he picked up a handful and said, 'Smells funny.' His partner, Johann, sniffed it and said, 'Too much chemical fertilizer, I think.' But I had stipulated absolutely no fertilizer. As the whole team was waiting to plant, Walter decided to cut it with bales and bales of peat moss. Huge holes were dug, the shrubs and trees planted and the perennial bed extended.

By autumn twelve of the shrubs were very dead and a large ten-by-six-foot patch in the perennial bed held nothing but dead plants; some of them were three-year-old phlox and delphinium, some deutzia shrubs. As I had no idea what I was dealing with, I dug out the whole patch and threw the earth away, then replanted using our own compost. However, I filled a plastic bag with the discarded topsoil, boxed it up and sent it to the University of Guelph. Their reply was tactful: 'Far, far too much fertilizer, but do you know whether or not the basic earth has come from a cornfield?'

Atrazine is an ingredient in a herbicide, which will destroy anything but corn. All the shrubs and some new trees were planted in it but they weren't all dead yet. Walter knows I hate what I call lollipop trees, and he had searched and found an elegant multi-trunked silver maple to place behind the trellis fence. It was fighting to live, and, determined to help it, I called around until I was finally referred to a first-class arborist. We had a long and horrifying conversation. He had once, he told me, been engaged to design and plant a two-acre garden, which he did, but unfortunately no one had told him that the two acres had been a cornfield for the prior five years. Everything died. He assured me that it is even possible to buy this frightful stuff in those charming and beautifully labelled plastic bags of potting soil for house plants. The nurseries have no more idea than we have that this is what they are using. Atrazine is not bio-degradable; but it is photo-degradable. If you keep turning it over and exposing it to light, it will eventually be gone though it may take two or three years.

The arborist's last piece of advice was, 'Don't buy topsoil. Make your own.'

How do you make your own topsoil? I sat down to think, and what I thought was—how could I have been so dumb? *Findhorn* told me, a herd of cows and four bales of oats told me, Doug said it, loud and clear: 'Two feet of topsoil.' We *had* been making it all along.

Of course, we had gone the wrong way about it.

What we should have done was till the front circle, remove the rocks, add manure and sow buckwheat. Buckwheat chokes out twitch and weeds. Till that down and sow rye and clover. Till again, plant again and till down until we had a deep bed of loam. That's called green-manuring. After that, and only after that, sow expensive grass seed. The same process should have been used on the vegetable garden. The two feet of topsoil that Doug had spread out could have been used as a 'bank' to be drawn on for flower beds, to plant the shrubs, but it was now planted to asparagus and raspberries.

So we knew how to make our own and we knew where to make it—out of sight and at the lowest point of the property, just before you walk into the cedars. There is access there from an old road, which Mr. McBride had used for hauling wood. Three plateaus leading off from that road would comprise nearly an acre. The farmer we asked to plow and disc in manure did his best to talk us out of it: 'You're wasting your money. Topsoil out of that stuff?'

But it's done. Once the rough part was over, Gordon tilled and sowed buckwheat. When it was about ten inches high, it was tilled down again and sown with rye. This spring, he'll till down and plant clover. It looks great already and can be brought to any part of the garden in small loads with our baby tractor and cart. As we remove it, we'll keep rebuilding with manure, leaves and grass plus weeds.

Topsoil and compost are all one. Topsoil is the slow accumulation of everything that dies; slow, because Nature takes her time. But, if we use our brains, we can speed up the process, creating that rich, crumbly cake I had found in the first garden.

You can make it in bins, heaps or holes, or right in the ground where you're going to use it. It's a miracle because, whether you're dealing with sand, clay or a gravel pit, it will give you a garden.

Food for Your Plants

Now I have to contradict myself. Topsoil and compost are not quite the same. One is chocolate cake and the other is devil's food cake or Black Forest cake, all depending on just how wickedly rich you make it. We use compost to mulch and feed the flower beds. Obviously, one can't be tilling and green-manuring a perennial bed or a rose bed. Renewing the earth in these depends on feeding and composting. The old books used to tell us to dig up a perennial bed every five years or so, put in fresh earth and replant, which is no doubt why they went out of fashion. Our herbaceous border is twelve years old and the earth grows livelier every year as compost is added to the top, spring and fall. Freezing and thawing, the rain and the earthworms carry it all down to the roots. The leaves are green, the flowers abundant and the stems strong, all of which testifies to the fact that the nitrogen, phosphorus and potash are in balance.

Determined to do something right the first time, I attended a lecture on how to make compost. This was Barbara's inspiration. Rather than depending on the instructions in our gardening books we were to go to the source, the man who made a fetish of compost heaps; we were to make notes, make diagrams, ask questions, then, bursting with knowledge, hand all the information over to our husbands, who would construct the bins. Mine were placed conveniently outside the vegetable garden. Chicken wire was wrapped around steel T-bars driven into the soil to make three adjoining bins, each a four-foot cube with the front left open. Three or four long wooden stakes were driven down into the soil inside each bin, which now awaited my expertise. In the first bin, I crossed corn stalks to make an airy base, then added six inches of green refuse, an inch of soil, a layer of wood ashes, a layer of bone meal and about three inches of cow manure. The layers were repeated in this order until the pile was four feet high, when the stakes were pulled out to create air shafts. The whole was moistened and topped with perforated black plastic.

The pile should then heat up. Once it has cooled down, the plastic is removed and the whole is forked, or turned into the next empty bin, and a new pile is built up in the first bin. By the time the original pile has spent the winter in the last bin, you should find dark, sweet-smelling compost. Barbara's had been built to the same recipe but neither hers nor mine had heated up, and what we found the following spring was an oily, gooey, unmanageable mess. I tilled ours into the vegetables garden anyway, and Barbara abandoned all thoughts of compost; but I had been raised on 'If at first you don't succeed, you're doing something stupid.'

In the first cleanup of the garden, not everything had made its way to the mound on the ridge. Old heaps had accumulated by the fence or behind a tree and turned into compost. Wherein lay the difference between these and our highly scientific heaps? No air shafts for one and no black plastic for another. What had we topped them with? Discarded turf.

We set to work again, building straight onto the soil base of the bins, layering as before and topping with turf, leaving a depression in the centre to catch rain and melting snow. Steam rose as the piles heated up, and what came out of the oven the following spring was deep brown, friable compost. They were never turned because we couldn't get at them for snow. When we ran out of turf in following years, we made the last layer earth and topped it with ten inches of hay mulch. One year we got fancy again and accumulated all the ingredients before we built the piles. They didn't heat up, and since then we have built the layers as we accumulate fresh green greens. Keep in mind that what works for us may not work for you, but if you experiment with this basic recipe you will find a formula that does. Nothing you can find in a plastic bag with a number on it can take its place. Compost is alive.

The bins, by the way, are closed with a barred wooden gate and face a platform of earth large enough for loading and turning the wheelbarrow. Place the bins near their point of use, or at least arrange things so that empty carts go uphill and full carts down. Sometimes the compost is too rough to go on a fine flower bed, in which case you screen it. We have made two screens of hardware cloth with wooden frames. One fits the top of the wheelbarrow and the other the top of the tractor cart. Throw the compost onto the screen with a shovel and rub it through with your gloved hands or a board. It sounds a dreary job, but everyone enjoys it. It looks so good, they say, and used as a mulch on a flower bed it's the handsomest stuff you ever saw.

Bone meal is our other standby, chiefly because the peonies, delphiniums and roses are so greedy for it. It won't burn plants and releases slowly. A great handful, sometimes two, is worked in by each plant, both spring and fall. The perennial bed and the vegetable beds get a thick dusting worked in at the same time. I now use steamed bone meal from a farmer's supply because it has less odour and works into the soil without caking.

Well-rotted cow manure top-dresses the asparagus bed but would look unsightly in the rest of the garden. There I use liquid sheep manure all summer, whenever the mood strikes, just in case something is feeling peckish. It's easy to make. Tie up several handfuls of treated sheep manure in cheesecloth; use a long string and tie the bag to the handle of a plastic garbage pail, medium size; fill with water and let the bag steep for a few days. You can dilute this liquid to the colour of weak tea to feed your roses and perennials especially.

If you have a fireplace, then you know that the wood ashes are potash, favourite food for delphiniums, anathema to slugs, and just what is needed to keep everything lively and dancing. Store it where it can't leach out.

'C Food' emulsion or seaweed powder I use mainly on the greenhouse plants once they are in the four-leaf stage; both are highly recommended for vegetables and even shrubs and trees.

None of the above foods will burn your plants or spur them into sudden, weak growth. They are slow but long-lasting and constantly improve your soil, keeping it in balance.

Study your plants. If they are sturdy and active with good root systems, there is nothing to worry about. Potash keeps your plants active, phosphate encourages fruit and flowers and nitrogen keeps them green. All of these ingredients are in natural balance in compost, so I don't resort to the chemical numbers system for fear of throwing everything out of whack. Nitrogen was built up in the soil when we green-manured with clover, phosphate we know is in our soil in plentiful supply and the potash is, as I've said, in the wood ashes. But there are many other substances—some known, some not—that the plants require. These could be affected by chemical fertilizers, and I hesitate to use them, just as I hesitate to take antibiotics or hand them out wholesale to the family. To put it another way, give your plants a meat, potatoes and vegetable meal, not pills and a TV dinner.

Food for the Family

Over the years in the vegetable garden we have used manure, tilled down all the residue of the season, green-manured with rye and/or buckwheat, then tilled again in spring. When we had about a fourteen-inch depth of topsoil we decided to try high, wide intensive planting. The theory is that you never have to till again. Fortunately, at the time, we had a good man helping out one day a week; he liked to work and he liked to dig. I set out the shape of the beds with stakes and string, then he shovelled all the soil out of the paths and tossed it into the beds. Some of the beds were silly. I had been trying to avoid a burial-ground appearance and had dotted in two three-foot squares, one for carrots, one for beets. With the palm of my hand I simply smeared beet seeds over the whole bed, sprinkled on compost and patted it down, just as our two-year-old had done long ago. (I'm a slow learner.) As fast as I harvested big fat beets off the top more pushed up from below. They appeared to be in tiers, four layers deep. It was the biggest beet crop we've ever had, and we were thoroughly sick of them by the time the last bunch was picked. All out of one square yard.

I tried something new with the carrots as well. The tiny seeds were mixed with sand, then planted with the smear method and left to grow and grow, with no radishes or anything else to thin them out. When the first carrots were about four inches I started to harvest. By that I mean I would grasp the tops and pull out two handfuls, enough for dinner. The tiny carrots were thrown on the compost and the rest, perfectly formed, were eaten. They pulled easily out of the loose soil, the big fellows late in the season were straight and true, and I had done no thinning at all. And no weeding, of course, because the planting was too thick to let weeds in.

Now we placed mulch only on the hard paths between the beds, lifting it up to tuck round the plants only where we found a bare place, and there were few of those because beans and peas had been planted thickly too. Only pre-started plants, lettuce and cauliflower, needed mulching.

The difficulty with this method is to keep the beds fertile. We top-dressed with bone meal, blood meal and compost, but the second season was only good, not spectacular. We had added a trickle irrigation system to make watering easier, and I wondered if all the good was being leached out into the paths or whether the weather was a factor.

The irrigation system shot off in all directions and, as it was easy to redesign, we decided to do just that. The new design made it simple to pull the lines back over the fence while the whole garden was tilled and re-shaped. Then the lines were set back in place.

It was a young farmer who came to make the newly-shaped beds, and he told us he used the same method but stacked mulch on top of all the beds before snowfall. The snow packs the earth down and leaches it, but the mulch keeps it high and fluffy; so we're trying it, and only next season will tell.

With the beds plotted in a permanent design it's easy to rotate, alternating root crops with leaf crops each year, but the strawberry beds stay in place for three years. Before they run out, daughter plants are lifted in August to start a new bed and aren't allowed to bear until the second season. (Nip the blooms off the first year.) Strawberries should not go back in the same bed for at least five years.

Every farmer knows about rotating food crops, but I was interested to read in *Victoria Sackville-West's Garden Book* that just possibly some flowers should be rotated as well. A few plants, which had thrived for years in one place, began to look sorry for themselves. Moved to a new place they perked up. My garden may not be old enough for that to have occurred as yet— though when I replace tulip bulbs after five years the new bulbs always go in a new place, and plants are forever being shifted as I try for a better effect, which may take care of the problem. At any rate, if a plant looks unhappy it may be a good idea to give it a new home. It may be just bored, a touch of shack fever. But peonies are stay-at-homes, and modern roses transplant with difficulty. Leave them be.

Seeds and the Two-Hundred-Dollar Greenhouse

Findhorn, so the book says, is a miracle. I'll believe that. Every garden is a miracle. A blade of grass is a miracle. The basic miracle, for every gardener, is the seed. When you hold one in your hand you may, if it is a tomato or cucumber seed, know what it is. Some you won't know. The thing is, *the seed knows.* Amazing! The secret of the universe is in there somewhere. The seed fashions itself into anything from an apple tree to a head of lettuce, and though I've read all that stuff about the DNA molecule, the genes, the messages for assembly going on between them, I really don't think I can believe any of it; the whole thing is a mystery and a wonder.

I ordered a packet of petunia seeds. When I peered into the little plastic bag there appeared to be nothing of anything much to be seen. More out of faith than aught else, I put in a teaspoon of sterile sand and sprinkled the whole over a flat of damp sterile earth. I never did that again. The petunias appeared so thickly that I had a long, anxious job of winkling them apart and setting them out in five separate flats and throwing the rest away. Now I plant as thinly and sparingly as I can manage.

But why involve yourself in growing your own when the professionals will do it for you? If your garden is small and you are happy with what sells well, that's fine. But in our case the garden was large: at least thirty large flats and innumerable small boxes of twelve were needed each season. As well, I wanted specific colours that I couldn't count on finding in the nurseries in sufficient quantity, and there were plants I couldn't find in the nurseries at all. But they were in the seed catalogues.

For years I ordered the greater quantity of my seeds from Stokes. Whatever little I know about seeds I learned from

Stokes. On the back of every packet you will find detailed and specific instructions for that particular seed. Some germinate in the dark at 50°F, others want light and an underneath temperature of 80°F, or mild light and a temperature of 60°F. Some should be frozen or soaked in water before planting. Stokes guided me through the maze.

One section of our basement is organized with old window screens set up on trestles. Each table holds ten big flats. Fluorescent lights (the kind designed to stimulate growth) that can be raised and lowered hang from chains above the tables. The temperature here is about 70°F, which suits the majority of seeds. Then the fun begins. The snapdragons are frozen in the freezer. A far dark corner of the basement floor is about 50°F and here I set a flat of verbena, wrapped in a black plastic bag. A basement window is 60°F and has a soft, filtered light, where the strawberries germinate. When I need underneath heat of nearly 80°F, the top of the refrigerator is the answer; but, as well, I have a box with a heating coil, covered with a little earth, and some flats are set in this. If you have a cold cellar for the storage of vegetables, this too is a great place for the seeds that want the dark and a cool temperature—delphiniums, for instance, after freezing.

I am not overly fond of plastic, but to avoid damp-off and create the sterile conditions required for success I have found plastic the easiest way to go. I bought quantities of ten-by-twenty-inch plastic flats, which come with drainage holes punched in. These wash clean, stack easily for storage and last about three seasons. Strips of peat pots are used for plants that should be transplanted with as little disturbance as possible, and my favourite pot for tomatoes is a styrofoam drinking cup. When the time comes to set them in the garden, I cut carefully round the cup, leaving about two inches at the top, slide the bottom of the cup off, and ease the two-inch top up along the stem. The root and part of the stem are planted deeply. The cup sits around the stem, anchored in earth, and foils the cut-worms waiting to nip the plant off at the base. (You can make paper collars, held with paper-clips, but it takes longer.)

Another note on preparing the flats: to dampen the earth for seeding, it's best to set the flats in water until all the earth is wet, then let them drain on the screen tables overnight. By then the earth is moist and ready for planting. When preparing the plant room, as I call it, I installed a deep laundry tub—to my regret, as it is exactly a quarter of an inch too narrow to allow me to set the trays in. A long shallow sink would have been preferable. I now use a long galvanized tin tray with sides three inches deep, fill this with water and use it for dipping trays. It does have the advantage of being transferable to the greenhouse. Once the trays are seeded they are covered with saran wrap. After much experimentation with clear plastic and glass tops, I find the saran less cumbersome.

This next ploy will meet with the violent disapproval of just about every gardener I know. Transplanting, they will say, strengthens the plant. I don't transplant until everything is moved into the garden. Every flat I need is planted thinly with seeds in three rows. When the true leaves (the second pair) appear, I lay a stick along each row. (The stick has a black mark every three inches.) Now, and this is like plucking eyebrows, I remove every seedling that is not sitting in front of a black mark. Result: one flat of thirty plants, evenly spaced, ten to a row. Sometimes, because I can't bear to throw them away, I will transplant some of the seedlings into a new flat. They don't grow one bit better than those that were left in place. As the plants develop they are fed with an organic liquid sea-food, unless another specific fertilizer is required.

Then the time comes—April, for me—when all the seedlings have to be moved away from the fluorescent lights and into a cooler temperature, about 55°F. If this is not done, the stems grow thin and long—'leggy' is what it is called—and what you want is a lot of fat, chunky little plants.

And that brings us to the greenhouse.

(Note: if you wonder why plants are started indoors, it's because there is a greater choice of temperatures and the plants like it. As I write this, it is the twelfth of March and snowing outside. I like it better indoors too.)

Greenhouse, Cold-frame or Both

When we really had to have a greenhouse—which was at the beginning, when there were great beds to be filled with plants—we were still staggering from the expense of building and decorating. There were four greenhouses that I could visit and inspect, all belonging to friends. Two were attached to the house and two freestanding. All were of glass, custom-built and very expensive.

Those attached to the house were clean, pretty and warm greenhouses; that is, they were suited to the culture of orchids, indoor and other tender plants. The other two were cool, for the cultivation of outdoor annuals and perennials, and there was lots of earth about, on the benches and the floor, because these were work-places, not show-places. In other words, did I want a clean greenhouse or a dirty greenhouse? Very few books on greenhouses raise this point. The other thought that gave me pause was that one of these elaborate structures didn't see a great deal of use. Would I grow bored with the thing and leave it standing idle?

It was then that I came upon an advertisement for a plastic greenhouse, for a mere two hundred dollars. The manufacturer was in California, but the whole kit could be shipped with instructions for assembly. It was spacious, which I needed, eight feet by twelve, and though it was supposed to perch upon the grass, Gordon thought he could anchor it to the ground. If it lasted for only one or two seasons it was worth it to find out if greenhousing was my thing. To my surprise, the manufacturer took a keen interest in the whole enterprise. Recognizing that we would be dealing with heavy snowfall, he recommended a ripple plastic of greater strength and asked us to place it out of the wind.

We tucked it in the service yard to the south of the garage wall. A slat floor was firmly anchored at the corners and down the long sides to T-bars driven deep into the ground; the redwood framing was fastened firmly to the two-by-fours of the floor. When the plastic was cut according to the detailed instructions I had a greenhouse. No, not yet: it had to be heated. At first we tried propane, an experiment that lasted only a month, as the propane truck was coming every three days and it cost more to heat than the main house. We had to switch to a small industrial electric heater, its thermostat set permanently to 55°F. When the four-foot trench from house to greenhouse was dug for the power line (we have to be below frost-line in these parts) Jon was home. 'Hold it,' said he, before we back-filled. 'Are you planning to trot back and forth from basement to green-house with watering cans?'

I was.

'Do you use cold or warm water?' Well, of course you must use lukewarm water on seedlings or they'll die of shock. So a plastic pipe was laid alongside the power line, and through that an ordinary plastic garden hose. One end is at the laundry tubs in the basement where it can be attached and the water temperature adjusted as I please; the other end is in the green-house, looped around a hook and long enough to reach in all directions. Now I really did have a greenhouse, and I realized why my friend had abandoned hers: she has to carry water to it from the house. Water, warm water, is as essential in the greenhouse as heat. Don't be without it.

The shelves, too, are plastic, with deep grooves so that air can get under the flats, and to allow them to drain after water-ing. Gordon put another shelf underneath on both sides, which gave me forty-eight feet of shelving. This was over ten years ago, and my temporary greenhouse is still there and still in use. We keep meaning to replace it with one of the new elegant affairs, but we now have less and less need for home-grown plants, as I concentrated on perennials long ago and the beds are bursting with plants I shall have to give away. Plastic has certain advantages. Hail bounces off it: no smashed glass. At the end of the season I clear the benches, turn on the water to scalding hot and hose down roof, walls, benches and floor. Now it's ready to store extra garden furniture. Before it's closed for winter I scald it down again. No problems with white-fly, wasps, baby snakes or damp-off.

One last word of caution: acquaintances attached a superb glasshouse off their dining room, facing south. This overheats the dining room to the point where it can't be used in the summer at all. The great problem with a greenhouse is keeping it cool, and though we have a large exhaust fan, we still need a slat screen over the south wall outside and a trellis fence in front of that. Even so, before the twenty-fourth of May it's so hot all the plants have to be lifted outdoors. (This should be done in any case to harden them off before planting.)

The other device for hardening off plants is a cold-frame. I suggest you explore all the alternatives here, from aluminum with automatic open-and-close tops to all the designs for do-it-yourself addicts, from concrete block to wood. They are ideal for the house with a small garden. In my first cold-frame I wintered-over delphiniums; they went in the size of tangerines and by spring were the size of footballs. I've been a cold-frame addict ever since. We now have six sets of collapsible wooden frames, which we can set at will over the vegetable beds. Whatever needs one, gets one. The hinged double top, which rests on a crossbar, can be flipped back for work or air. Another advantage is that your plants are placed where you want them to grow. When they are mature, you can move the frames, not the plants. We got very fancy and added screens to break heavy rain on tender seedlings. For us, the great thing is that they fold and stack and can be put away for winter. But the alternatives here are so varied that, as I've said, you're better to do your own detective work.

Perennials

I can't leave the subject of seeds without talking about perennials. I had been converted long ago by Helen Van Pelt Wilson with her marvellous book: *Perennials Preferred*. I do indeed prefer them because they become old friends, whereas the annuals come and go. When I started this country garden I had found only one grower of perennials, and these were such sad, small, moth-eaten objects, I felt they would never survive. When they did I would discover, to my aggravation, that the lovely white drift I had planned was pink or fuschia. And the blues were rarely blue: they were mauve or purple. Now I have found a grower who is as enthusiastic about perennials as I am. If you live anywhere near Toronto, his name is Keith Squires; his nursery is on Steeles Avenue West and is called The Country Squire's Garden. He has one foible: everything is in Latin. I have to study for an hour before I can talk to him on the phone and for two if I go in to buy.

However, in the early stages I had no choice but to turn to the seed catalogues and grow my own. The catalogues are confusing if you are not a knowledgeable gardener, but you will find a few old friends and meet others by bravely ordering the seeds and raising them yourself. Or—and this is faster—visit your nearest botanical gardens in June and take colour photographs of the plants that appeal to you. They are all labelled. If you number the photos and keep a list of the names by number, you can make up your own album of plants, learning the Latin names into the bargain. Then all you have to do is find the seeds!

We did this at the botanical gardens in Montreal. The most successful find for me was *Oenothera missouriensis*. (I bought the plants, not seeds.) Penstemon came beautifully from seeds and lasted only one season. Some, *Coreopsis verticillata* and sidalcea, I haven't found as yet, but at least I know what I'm looking for. Finding the right nursery or the right seed-house is as big a piece of sleuthing as finding the plants.

I started the perennial border with three old friends: peonies, delphiniums and phlox. The peonies were ordered from Wild's of Missouri. Bringing them through customs was a saga in itself; but when I got them home and opened the still-moist moss in which they were wrapped, it was worth twice the exasperation. I had ordered six-eye roots: these were ten- and twelve-eye. They bloomed the first year and are now the joy of my life. A hedge of Festiva Maxima is a snowstorm of bloom in front of the trellis fence in the side garden by June, a lush green background after. As well, I like peonies as a centre for the line of perennials in the border.

Find a place for peonies, choose the best, order the biggest and place them where they're going to be forever. No, don't go chopping them up every three years. How ridiculous. Just give each a great handful of bone-meal and treated manure, spring and fall, and side-dress with compost. They love to eat. I support mine with four-ring wire cages intended for tomato plants. The leaves soon cover the cage and it is strong enough to support the immense heads.

I have less luck with the delphiniums. The plant that came riding in on Mary's mock orange is a blue I had never seen before and, try as I will, have not been able to find since. Hot on its trail, I grew from seed every blue in the Pacific Giants series and then the Blue Fountain. They were very lovely but not what I was searching for.

I grew dianthus one year, and out of the whole packet, one was different from all the others. This one exception, blue-green, perked up neatly all season, whereas all its sisters, grey-green, flopped and trailed after blooming. Walter said, 'Keep the good one and take divisions from it. Throw the rest out. You'll often get one plant out of a package of seed better than all the rest.' That may explain the delphinium of the enchanting blue; perhaps I should take seeds from it, though if it is a hybrid they won't germinate.

The main delphinium problem is that the moment they bloom we are struck with heavy rains or high winds, and the heavy flower heads snap over above the stake. The other is that they die down and leave a great hole in the perennial border. I thought I had solved this. At the beginning of May I scattered cosmos seed in two shades of rose around the delphinium plants, and when the delphs died down the cosmos were tall and generous in their place. At the second blooming I thinned out some of the cosmos and let the tall blue spires up through again. But the second season, to my dismay, the cosmos had seeded themselves all through the border. Hours were spent weeding them out. Foxglove and Canterbury bells are tall and lovely but bloom at the same time. Perhaps late-blooming lilies or the tall aster Improved Harrison's Pink? The real problem is

Photographs by: John Bentham Photography (top); Gordon Keeble (bottom)

Photograph by John Bentham Photography

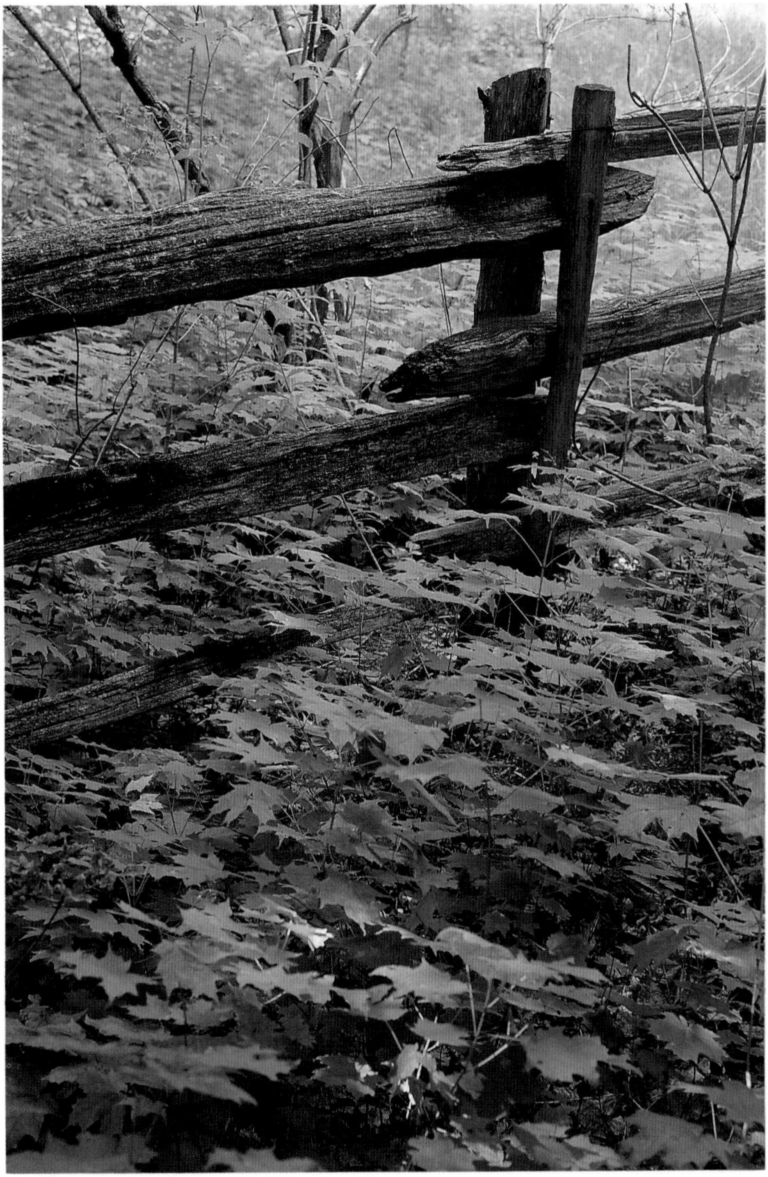

Photographs by John Bentham Photography

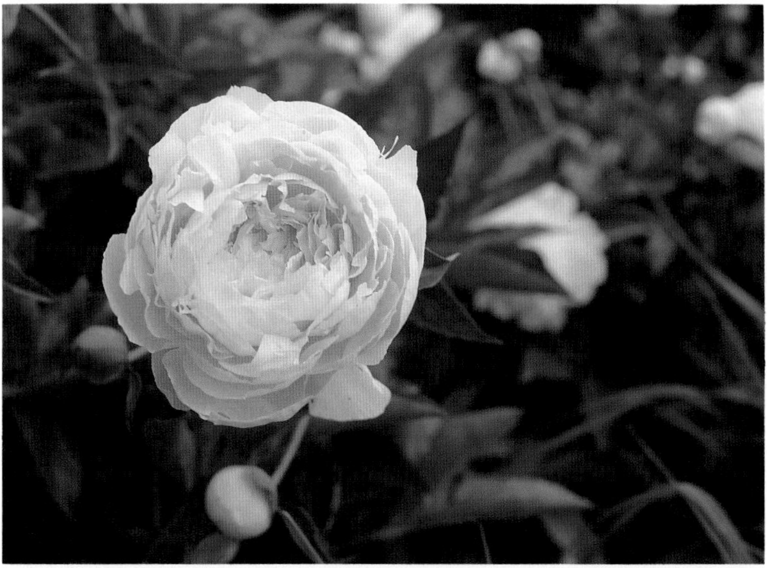

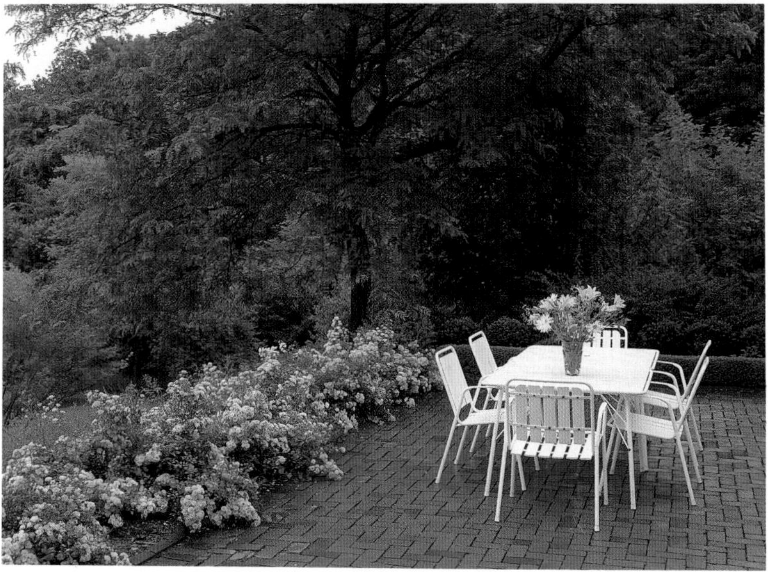

Photograph by John Bentham Photography

that I am trying to grow four- and five-foot plants right in the path of the wind.

Rugosa roses are now planted to the north of them to act as a windbreak, and if that doesn't prove to be a success I may give up. No, I can't do that.

Phlox I bought as plants, but the best are those given to me by friends, in the lively rose that I adore. Pale, washed-out mauve is not for me. White phlox is a great addition to the perennial border, cool on hot summer days, and I hope these will be ready for division soon. They grew to splendid size after the porcupine nipped them off. If they suffer at all from mildew, they are sprayed sparingly with Benomyl, which takes care of that and, apparently, porcupines.

Irises (also from Wild's) grow in their own bed, tumbling downhill just to the south of the back terrace. They are so tall that the blooms are visible above the four-foot wall, but once these are gone and all is spiky leaves they are out of sight. They had been in a bed of partial shade and had stopped blooming. Their new home is Walter's inspiration, and, of course, they were cleaned up and divided before replanting. Keep manure away from them, by the way.

These are my oldest and treasured friends. Of the new friends I don't know which delight me more: the McKana Giant columbines, the coral heuchera, the shasta daisies, the Rheingold pansies, or the salmon pink poppies, which come back smiling every year. White foxglove and Canterbury bells came and went and I must look them up again.

The heuchera brought me another friend. From a single packet of seeds I had enough plants to edge a forty-foot stone walk down the east side of the house, both sides. Then I took divisions to edge the bed of the side terrace. They grow in a low, neat mat of green, from which tall fronds covered with tiny coral bells rise and float about in the breeze. These lured the tiny ruby-throated hummingbird into the side or herb garden, which is directly beneath the east kitchen window. Here I can stand, oblivious to the work I'm doing at the sink, and watch this infinitesimal emerald-green jewel darting, hovering and weaving among the coral flowers, as lilliputian as he is. He has it all to himself after a minute but fierce aerial battle with another hummingbird who tried to invade the territory. (To tell the truth, they moved so fast I don't really know which was the victor.)

Grow heuchera both for itself and for the extra treasures it will bring. For the rest, you must choose your own friends.

Fair-weather Friends

Here today and gone tomorrow but nice to have around are the annuals. We had so much bare ground to cover at the beginning that every year I grew fourteen to fifteen flats of petunias, ten of snapdragons and fifteen more of whatever else came to mind.

Petunias and I parted first, more their choice than mine. Pink Cascade petunias were a heavenly shade in Nancy C.'s garden, but in mine they were burned and blown to tatters, and their place was taken by whatever could stand up to the sun and the wind. The snapdragons stayed longer. Particularly successful were the azalea-flowered Madame Butterfly and its small cousin, Sweetheart, and these have a special purpose.

The leaves of both narcissus and tulips must be allowed to die down and almost rot before you remove them in mid-July or you will have no flower the following year. Once they are gone they leave an empty space in the border, which is why many gardeners lift bulbs and, leaves still attached, heel them into the vegetable garden. Others, more profligate, throw them out and plant new bulbs every fall. I plant mine where other plants will screen them during the doldrums. Once the leaves are removed, I fill the space with snapdragons, which have been started late and held back for this planting.

An easier replanting can be done with the seeds you sow in place in April. Tickle the earth around the tulip and daffodil leaves and pat in lavatera or godetia. They interfere less with the ripening bulbs and can be thinned to fill the spaces gracefully. Both are delicate and enchanting flowers.

I am glad I grew perennials from seed. They require a little more trouble and tender loving care than annuals, but they grow to the stage where they stand on their own feet and you do little more than applaud and admire.

NOTES FOR THE NOVICE

Germination of Seeds

The following chart shows the germination requirements for some of the species most commonly grown from seed. But first, a few explanations:

NAMES: Plants are listed the way you are most likely to find them in the seed catalogues.

TOTAL DARK: Easily achieved by sliding flat into black plastic bag.

DO NOT COVER: Means press or firm seed into soil with board or fingertips. (Some seeds need light to germinate.) However, cover all flats with saran wrap or glass to keep in moisture until germination. Remove cover at first sign of green.

WATERING: Mist seedlings or lower flat into water container. Always use warmish water: 60 to 65°F (16–18°C).

TEMPERATURE: Temperatures given are for soil, but if plants were this fussy, nothing would germinate! Most of my seeds germinate in a room heated to 70 to 72°F (21–22°C) and under growth-stimulating fluorescent lights. Those wanting less than 60°F (16°C) for germination go into the cold cellar. For over 70°F (21°C), place on a heating cable.

Be sure you have *fresh*, viable seeds from a first-class seed house, then use clean flats and sterile soil.

When seedlings have their second set of true leaves, they are moved to a greenhouse to be held at 55 to 60°F (13–16°C) for growing on. Your greenhouse can give different temperatures if you test lower shelves and north and south walls; so will the windows of your house, or a cold-frame.

For really detailed instructions, turn to a good seed-house catalogue.

NAME	UNDER LIGHTS					OUTDOORS	
	GERMINATION TEMPERATURE	COVER	DO NOT COVER	GROW ON AT	SHADE	SOME SHADE	SUN
ALYSSUM	75°F (23°C), 10 days		*	55°F (13°C)		*	
AQUILEGIA (Columbine) McKana's Giant	Chill at 40°F (4°C), 5 days. Germ. 70-80°F (21-27°C), 21 days.		*	68°F (20°C)		*	
ASTER	70°F (21°C)	1/8" (3mm)		60°F (16°C)			*
BEGONIA, FIBROUS	70°F (21°C)	Sand thinly	14 hrs. light per day	65°F (18°C)		*	
CALENDULA (Scotch or Pot Marigold)	75°F (23°C), 20 days	1/4" (6mm) total dark, 10 days		65°F (18°C)			*

NAME	UNDER LIGHTS				OUTDOORS		
	GERMINATION TEMPERATURE	COVER	DO NOT COVER	GROW ON AT	SHADE	SOME SHADE	SUN
CAMPANULA (Bellflower)	70°F (21°C), 14 days	¹/₈″ (3mm)		60°F (16°C)		*	*
CARNATION	Freeze 7 days.	¹/₈″ (3mm)		60°F (16°C)	*		*
Annual	Alternate 70-60°F (21-16°C), 7 days						
Perennial	Nov. 1, 55°F (13°C)	¹/₈″ (3mm)		50°F (10°C)	*		*
CHRYSANTHEMUM Annual	Mar. 1, 60°F (16°C)	¹/₈″ (3mm) total dark, 10 days		60°F (16°C)			*
Perennial	70°F (21°C), 25 days		*		*		*
Shasta Daisy	Jan.-Feb., 60°F (16°C)		*	60°F (16°C)	*		*
COREOPSIS	75°F (23°C), 20 days	*			*		*

					Outdoors at 75°F (23°C), ¹/₄″ (6mm) deep
COSMOS					*
DELPHINIUM	Freeze 24 hrs. Feb., 55-65°F (13-18°C) for germination	¹/₈″ (3mm) lightly		60°F (16°C) day, 50°F (10°C) night	*
DIANTHUS Annual	70°F (21°C), 10 days	¹/₈″ (3mm)		50°F (10°C)	*
Perennial	Freeze 14 days, 70°F (21°C)	¹/₈″ (3mm)		60°F (16°C)	
DIGITALIS (Foxglove)	Feb. in pots, 70°F (21°C)		*	65°F (18°C)	*
HEUCHERA (Coral Bells)	3 seeds to pot, 70°F (21°C)	*		70°F (21°C)	*
IBERIS (Candytuft)	70°F (21°C), 7 days	*		50°F (10°C)	*

NAME	UNDER LIGHTS				OUTDOORS		
	GERMINATION TEMPERATURE	COVER	DO NOT COVER	GROW ON AT	SHADE	SOME SHADE	SUN
IMPATIENS	70°F (21°C)		*	65°F (18°C) shaded	*		
LARKSPUR							*
					Outdoors, late fall or spring after frost		
LAVANDULA (*Lavender*)						*	*
					Outdoors in May		
LAVATERA					*	*	*
					Outdoors, late May, warm soil		
MARIGOLD African or Dwarf Triploids	75-80°F (23-27°C)	$1/4 - 1/8''$ (6-3mm)		60°F (16°C)			*
MYOSOTIS (*Forget-me-not*)						*	
					Outdoors, June to August		

NICOTIANA (Flowering Tobacco)	75°F (23°C), 14 days		*	70°F (21°C)		* / Outdoors in mid-May
PANSY Swiss Giant	Chill 24 hrs. at 40°F (4°C). Total dark at 75°F (23°C), 10 days	1/8″ (3mm) sand		65°F (18°C)	*	*
PETUNIA	80°F (27°C) bottom heat, Dec.		*	60-65°F (16-18°C)	*	*
POPPY, ORIENTAL						* / Outdoors in peat pots at 75°F (23°C). Don't cover seed. Cover flat with black plastic, 10 days.

NAME	UNDER LIGHTS				OUTDOORS		
	GERMINATION TEMPERATURE	COVER	DO NOT COVER	GROW ON AT	SHADE	SOME SHADE	SUN
PRIMULA (Primrose)	Chill 48 hrs. at 40°F (4°C). 70°F (21°C), 40 days		*	60°F (16°C)	*	*	
ANTIRRHINUM (Snapdragon)	Freeze 48 hrs. Sow at 70°F (21°C), 7 days		* Press in 1/3" (3mm)	50°F (10°C) shade		* Pinch back	*
SWEET PEAS					* Pre-soak overnight. Plant in cold ground, April. Prefer heavy soil and broken shade.		
VERBENA	Total dark, 50-70°F (10-21°C), 20 days	1/8" (3mm)		50°F (10°C)		*	*
ZINNIA							* Outdoors mid-June, soil temp. 70°F (21°C).

The Pool

The summers here are as extreme as the winters, with temperatures soaring into the nineties, dry as dust, until the sky is suddenly rent with lightning, thunder and driving rain. But it was the heat and the dust that persuaded us, as I have said earlier on, that we mattered more than plans, gardens or budgets. Throwing all caution to the wind, we had decided to install a swimming pool. We knew where we wanted it: it should be below the house on the next plateau to the southwest, so that we could see its cool blue even when we weren't in it. We collected pictures and knew exactly how it should look: as much like a field pond as we could make it. Then it should have a pool-house or cabana with a great spreading roof to give us longed-for shade. All the wet feet, bathing suits and towels were to be down there, two hundred feet from the house.

We do learn a few tricks as time goes by, so we didn't tell any of the pool designers who called what we wanted. We let them tell us what they wanted. To a man, they wanted to use up the last level bit of land behind the house, then cantilever the pool out over the edge of the hill and use the basement for changing. We thanked them very much and said we would let them know.

It was a cold, rainy day when a young woman called to see me, armed with a large album of pictures of pools her firm had built. At the beginning we ignored the outside and looked at the album. Very pretty city pools. While I was making coffee, she suddenly called, 'Oh look, that's where your pool should go.' I came back to find her standing at the living-room window, pointing down to the second plateau. 'It shouldn't be oblong but a sort of wavy shape like a natural pond.' She started drawing pictures with her hands, like Walter. I showed her the pictures I had of pools in fields, with great rocks at the edges. We already had the rocks, stacked helter-skelter by the cedar-rail fence. We drank gallons of coffee in complete accord: it helps if the designer is on your side to start with.

She went off with my pictures to show to her boss. Then we were in trouble. He'd never heard of such a thing—not in this climate. He wanted a deeply reinforced deck to protect the pool from cracking in our severe weather. But, inch by inch, he came round to our way of thinking in the main essentials. Now this may or may not surprise you, but you can have a pool any shape you want at no extra expense if it's poured concrete with a mar-bleite finish. Stakes were set out in a forty-by-twenty-foot shape and rope strung round them. They placed the stakes, and when they were gone I went up to the house and looked down from the terrace, from bedroom windows, every angle I could think of. Then I went down, hauled out stakes and rearranged until I had a shape that looked less like a bent sausage and fit the plateau. When they came back they liked it. With no more ado, the hole was excavated to that meandering shape, deep at the diving end and rising briskly to three feet at the shallow. If you are one of those swimmers who want to do forty laps every morning and know exactly the distance you want to put in, this is not for you. We like ours because it's never boring: you can swim to the far bay, float on your back down the long, curving side and then nose under to the waterfall.

The waterfall is one immense rock with others placed round it. A hole was drilled through the big rock with a jackhammer, then the water from the filter taken underground and back through the rock. Warm water bubbles out of the hole and spreads out on a fan-shaped rock before returning to the pool. The diving-rock is an oddly-shaped eight-inch-thick piece of granite, which rests on the fieldstone deck and extends out over the pool by only ten inches. No, it does not bounce up and down, but no one seems to mind, and my grandsons appear to be able to flip in from it in every style but a swan dive.

Other rocks, of interesting shapes and textures (two are like fat pillows covered with lichen) and an immense platform rock, filled with ancient fossils, are placed round the deck. To my surprise, they are hot in the sun, and everyone sits and sizzles on them to dry off. You will gather there is, much against my wishes, a deck. It was 'no deck, no pool', and I lost. The contractors did their best, waved its outline to accent the pool, allowed an extending edge over the water, and left planting pockets beside the big rocks set down in the fieldstone. I object, too, to the tile on the inner edge, the white lining of marbleite, and most particularly to the chrome ladder, but that is removable. If ever the deck begins to collapse with age, I can go back to the idea of the farm pond, but may have collapsed myself by then.

There were problems. Always there are problems. First and foremost, the company insisted on using their landscape man. Walter, when called, said, 'I know him. He's good. Don't worry and carry on. Besides, he has the equipment for moving those rocks.'

Our rocks were left behind by the glacier a million years or more ago and, about a hundred years ago, were pulled out of the ground and placed on the boundary line by Mr. McBride before he planted his apple trees. Mr. McBride knew what he was doing. The wooden stone boats they used then are on display in the Royal Ontario Museum. The day came when I longed for Mr. McBride.

The landscape firm had a truck with a crane. I pleaded with them to drag the rocks down over the hill, warned that they were dense and heavy; but no, they lifted them with the crane and then drove downhill. I didn't want to look and hid inside the house. The smaller rocks went down without incident, but when I heard all the shouting I ran, in spite of myself, to the window. The big waterfall rock was on the crane, and truck and rock were see-sawing on the hill, first one off the ground, then the other. I prayed that the driver would jump free and then, to my vast relief, the crane snapped in two and the rock rolled downhill to its new home all by itself. They were all very cheerful about it, and I am sure it all turned up on our bill.

They installed five mature maples and a locust for shade. All else I firmly handed back into their truck. Inspect the plants commercial firms bring you. These were so weak, tired and infested with bugs, it would have been better to pay them to take them away. I had bugs. Millions of them. Why buy more?

The trees were so mature that we never thought to protect them and paid for our ignorance the following spring when we found three out of the six completely girdled by rabbits—the bark had been chewed away in a ring around the trunk, leaving an eight-inch band of bare wood. The thin layer of cambium just beneath the bark carries food from the roots to the leaves; the leaves in turn, by means of photosynthesis, manufacture nourishment for the roots. Once this circulatory system is cut, the tree dies. Three of our trees died. A fourth, partially girdled, had been left with a narrow vertical band of bark still in place. We painted the bare wood with orange shellac to seal off the weeping of sap, stood back and waited. Not only did the tree survive, but today it is impossible to see where the injury was made.

Another problem I wouldn't mention except that friends who have installed pools have faced the same thing. You order the pool in winter, oblivious to the fact that everyone else is ordering too, and when spring comes the contractor goes mad trying to get them all in, having promised each customer that he's first in line. Don't count on swimming until the first cool days of September. They start it, then you wait. Reacting to your frantic calls, they do a little more. All that still doesn't excuse the fact that the crew to spray the marbleite and the crew to lay the sod around the deck arrived on precisely the same day, when they had had all the days in three months to choose from. One crew was Portuguese and the other crew Italian, both highly volatile. As the soil blew in on the marbleite it became clear that blood would be shed. As loud shouts of indignation were exchanged with equally loud shouts of defiance, the noise attracted the attention of Bill, our carpenter, who was quietly applying cedar shakes to the cabana roof. Bill wouldn't look sideways if a bomb went off in his ear, and he now slowly descended the ladder and ambled into the melee, hammer idly swinging in one hand. As he talked, first one and then another of the spray crew went off to sit under the apple trees. Seeing what he was up to, I dashed down with offers of coffee and at length the marbleite crew were all having a very happy morning, relaxing in the shade, at nine dollars per hour per man. The grass was set in place, the deck was hosed off and that crew departed. In the peace and quiet of the afternoon, the marbleite was sprayed on and that group departed, with expressions of enthusiastic affection all round.

Now all that could be heard was the tap of Bill's hammer. I went down and said, 'Thanks Bill.'

'Nearly had a war,' he chuckled.

'Would you like a coffee?'

'Nope. Got to finish this.'

'Bill? I've built a new house to look like an old house. I could have bought an old house.'

'The rooms wouldn't be where you want 'em and it wouldn't be here.'

'Ah. But now I've built a pool, trying to make it look like a pond—I could have had a farm pond here.'

'If you like lots of company.'

'I like company.'

'Toads? Snakes? Leeches? Ponds are all mud and reeds on the bottom . . . you can't see.' He gave all his attention to lining up another shingle, letting me know that I was interrupting a man at his work.

As I climbed back up the hill, I counted my blessings.

Farm ponds, the genuine article, are more popular here where people have livestock—cows, ducks and so forth. Some are large enough for a rowboat and are stocked with trout. One family, who have both a pool and a pond, tell me that the pond is much nicer to swim in if you don't mind cold water and lots of company—the aforesaid frogs, snakes and whatnot.

Our pool is a little of both. The main thing to keep in mind is that it can be designed to fit the shape and character of your garden. You don't have to have a great rectangle unless a great rectangle is what you want.

Pulling It All Together

Once the pool was in, we discovered we had a series of unrelated islands: the house, the vegetable garden, the front circle and the pool on its own plateau. The drive and the paths, plus the pool road, were being churned up by everyone's feet, by cars, carts and trucks. The driveway that swept past the front door was the first problem. Mud tracked in, but that was the least of it. Rain ran from the top in a torrent and ended up in the garage. The cars were standing in four inches of water. When this froze we really were marooned. We brought in a 'dozer operator and asked him to drop the grade nine inches at the bank so the water would run off there; the next time it rained we had three inches of water. We had it graded again and were down to two inches of water.

I called in another firm. The boss arrived and I explained our difficulties. 'Your problem,' said he, 'is that you don't know how to drive a bulldozer.' Before I could raise a hackle, he doubled up his fist and left the centre knuckle out in a nasty little triangle. 'Can you do that?'

I showed him that I could do that.

'Good. Now, when my driver arrives, I want you to climb up to the cab and pound him on the head with that until you get his attention. Always. Get their attention.'

When a nice red-headed young man arrived, mounted high up on the 'dozer, I clenched my fist as instructed and told him what his boss had had to say. He beamed down and gave me a little bow. 'Lady. You have my attention.'

'Right.' I then drew a line across the drive leading to the bank. 'I want you to dig a trench right there, nine inches deep.'

'But . . . ' I waved my pointy fist and he cut the trench.

'Now, I want you to drop the blade and feather back from

that side of the trench all the way to the top of the hill. When that's done, come round this side and feather back to the doors of the garage.'

'Oh, I get it! But why didn't you just say you wanted it graded to a nine-inch drop?' I smiled. 'You tried that before, eh?'

'Twice.'

Now, when it rains, it's a pleasure to watch the water swoosh down the hill and out over the bank. (Mr. Biles says, when grading, start at the low point and work up to the high point.)

Head swollen with success, I decided to explain this to the next two who came—two Irishmen, father and son. They were going to lay a stone court across the front of the house and a path down the side. As these were next to the house, they had to drain away from it. About half the stone was out of the truck when I started to tell them what I wanted. The father was standing holding a four-inch-thick piece of flagstone weighing about two hundred pounds. As I talked, he put it back in the truck, gave his son a nod and they both were reloading. 'What are you doing?'

'Going home. If any woman thinks she can tell me . . . ' He was still holding a large stone, and I retreated into the house.

'Gooordon!'

Gordon said, 'Make coffee,' and walked casually out of the door. As the coffee brewed, I peered out the window to see Gordon and the Irishman sitting on a pile of rocks, talking and occasionally laughing. I wondered what they were talking about—women, probably. I served them coffee, eyes downcast and meek as a mouse.

The stone was laid, starting at the high point and working down. Against all the rules, he graded as he went along. It was a fine job and, of course, it drains. Sometimes a stone will lift with frost but it settles right back into place.

This type of court can have various openings for low plantings in the English style. They take away from the commercial look and are cool and inviting in summer. The court joined a stone path of the same material leading around the corner down the east side of the house, between house and side garden. This gave us a six-foot-deep bed along the house and a twenty-by-fourteen-foot garden for herbs. Now that the driveway drained and was topped with limestone, we could walk dry-shod from car or garage to both the front and the kitchen door. We have become so used to this that now in spring and fall, when driving out to friends' homes, we have to remind ourselves to wear boots because our host's driveway will probably be mired in mud. When friends call on us they stop on the front porch and say, 'It's dry out there. How do you do that?' I give them the phone numbers and no instructions.

Now I needed Walter and phoned to tell him so. I heard him drive up on a sunny morning, but he didn't come to the door. I waited and waited, thinking he wanted to walk about on his own. When at last he knocked and I opened the door, he was wearing a big smile. 'I've been inspecting your greenhouse.'

I quailed, knowing it was stuffed with plants in full flower, crying out to be planted. 'I give you an A,' said Walter and we both went out to look; me, very pleased with myself.

Walking through a garden with Walter is an extraordinary experience. He sees everything, every leaf, twig and bud. And bug. The running commentary and quick snippets of advice are accompanied by the ever-present secateurs, showing you how to prune and where, what's happy and what isn't, and all the time the general design is coming to life: a big group of trees there, shrubs there, steps here. He lets the land tell him.

Every property requires its own design to suit the land, to suit the house, to suit you, so that if I gave you ours it wouldn't help much. If you are not sufficiently skilled to do it yourself, go to all lengths to find the man or woman whose ideas march with your own. It takes a professional eye, but some professionals can make a property look like a well-kept grave or the front of an insurance building. When you see a garden that really appeals to you, knock on the door and ask the owner who designed it. He'll be flattered. What I'm saying is, find your own Walter. When he was finished, it had all come together and looked as though it had been there all along. It wasn't planned on graph paper, but we knew what we were getting because he could turn himself into a tree or shrub and make us step back and look. When the real trees arrived they were set in place, and we stepped back to look from all angles before they went into the ground. A flat piece of paper can't give you this view.

Here, the general principle was to group trees and shrubs the way they would naturally plant themselves, but allowing a little more space. No straight lines. Even our paths took the way of least resistance, curving because the land curves. The steps (railway ties, staggered in twos or threes) went down the hill following a natural gully, probably an old stream bed. Low plantings here and there anchored the paths to the ground.

When I complained that the perennial border looked too small and 'stuck on', Walter swung one end deep back into the lawn and anchored it with a blue spruce, encircled with low evergreens. In time the evergreens will come out and the spruce will spread its wide skirts to the ground. Here is the background for the delphiniums. The far end was balanced with a crabapple spreading its branches in blessing over the plants beneath.

Once the shape was there and accented, we realized it had been there all along. It just took a pro to see it.

What follows is a walk through my garden. You won't want to copy it. There are parts you will think I could improve on. Oh, I think so, too! But you might pick up an idea here and there and if you're like me, nosing about other people's gardens is a pleasant experience. Let's start at the front.

The Perennial Border

As you know by now, the perennial border is where it is because that's where the farmer dumped the cow manure. It should properly have been placed against a background—a fence, a stone wall, something to protect it and set it off. But now, when I drive in, I like to see it curving out to greet me. And when I step out the front door, I like to see it curving back and spread out in all its splendour. The Elizabethans named this sort of planting the Garden of Pleasure and Delight. That's a little high-falutin for me, but I do see their point, for here I spend my happiest hours.

All arguments to the contrary, perennials are a lot less work than annuals. This border, a long curve of eighty feet, now eighteen feet deep in places and twenty at its centre, is not a back-breaking chore. It receives two days' attention spring and fall, when it is cleaned up and fed. Apart from that, an hour or so once a week, taking out dead heads and holding converse with the residents, is more a pleasure than a task. Granted, at the beginning the weeding was monumental, but we started with a five-foot depth and have gradually worked our way back, cleaning out grass and mulching as we go. I had promised myself that when I was seventy I would erase all but the peon-ies. However, when the moment arrived, I called Walter and said now that I was seventy, I'd changed my mind. 'That border is too shallow, let's go for twenty feet depth and add roses and shrubs.' Walter kept saying, 'You're *what*?' and came the next day, feeling that not a moment should be lost. Perennial borders are the glory of a garden. If I can do it, you can do it.

Because this border stands free and is visible from the back, the front and the sides, it has developed into a double border: the almost-L shape is a help, as is the depth. The high line toward the back is the rugosa roses and five-foot shrubs. Behind them, in slight shade, are columbine, pansies, lobelia and any other small types who like it there.

In front of the rugosas on the south side, and at the tall end in front of the blue spruce, there is a drift of blue delphinium, leading centre to a drift of white phlox, then deep rose phlox. These are faced down with peonies, Red Charm, Jules Elie, and the creamy single with the golden anthers, Carrara. Tall single lilies for accent are in there and the day lilies, Vesper and Hyper-ion, waiting for the hot July days. All these tallish types are faced down with shorter plants—blue dwarf campanula, white peach bellflower (*Campanula persicifolia*), thrift, Ozark sundrop (*Oenothera missouriensis*)—and right at the front, drifting into the garden and down over the grey curb of loose fieldstone, is arabis. I said I was a greedy gardener. The border is divided at the centre by fieldstone, planted with creeping thyme. The planting on the right repeats in its essentials that on the left, and both curved ends have shasta daisies.

There is a reason for such a variety of plants: each has its season, and you want waves of bloom. In May, the white bloom of arabis accents the tulips and daffodils, and the garden is full of promises, promises. June, you will recall, is when things are busting out all over and gardeners invite their friends to come and see the luscious globes of peony, the delicate columbine, the paper-petalled poppies with dramatic black centres, and the deep blue delphiniums, thrusting up their spires to join the regal lilies. They don't, of course, all burst into bloom on the same day but come on stage as they please. There are troughs between the waves when the peonies die down and all else is in bud but not in flower. There is no colour, and you find yourself with a bad case of 'the garden was simply beautiful last Tuesday'. Never mind. Real gardeners know all about it. It happens to them too.

Day lilies arrive in midsummer (July) as delphinium dies down and you are trimming back the pansies and columbine. Phlox appear to combine their white, salmon and pale rose with the gold of the day lily. One hopes the blues of campanula and balloon flower are in there as well.

Plan for August, leaving space for late blooming phlox or Michaelmas daisies. If you have tucked in the late day lilies, Autumn King and Harvest Sunshine, you may achieve a great shout of golden trumpets—to announce the spectacular of the year, when all the woods turn to scarlet and bronze.

If gardening is new to you, all the above will sound as dull as a dinner party where everyone talks about people you've never heard of. All you can do is get around more. Look at the catalogues with the colour pictures and tour the nurseries where all the plants are labelled. If you buy a few and try them out, you'll soon begin to know them even with their incredible Latin names.

The Side Garden

Now we walk down the east side of the house. On our right is a six-foot-deep bed. At first irises were planted here, but they had only the morning sun and were shaded by the house the rest of the day. What began as a small green mystery from Mary's house has now developed into a hedge of baby's breath flat against the wall. But it isn't baby's breath. It stays stiff and tall through all weathers and has a leaf like woodruff. But it's too tall for woodruff. When the sweet peas bloom, I say it's baby's breath and tuck it into bouquets. Day lilies are in front, and on both sides of the kitchen door are the plantings of Christmas rose (*Helleborus niger*). The bed is edged with heuchera, which leaves a twelve-inch space between edging and day lilies. What do you think would be pretty in there? Anemone? Monkshood? No, begonias blew to bits. Have to think.

While I've been thinking, the hellebores have made the decision for me. If you look closely, you will see that three have seeded themselves, two-leaf seedlings, which at this early stage can be carefully lifted and lined out where they choose to grow or into a flat for later placement.

The other side of the path is an oblong twenty feet long by fourteen deep. When we first came here the architect urged us to close in some part of the garden: 'With all this space you'll feel as if you're falling off the world. Have an outside room.'

So here is our public-secret garden. Gordon made an eight-foot trellis or lattice fence, which I wanted carried round the whole space. I was talked out of that by 'you'll spoil the view!' friends, so part of it was reduced to four feet. Fortunately, it needs replacing now, and it's going to be fence all round as soon as we can get to it. An outside room is an outside room. As it is, it isn't—if you follow.

You want to be able to sit down in a room and the herb jungle had to be curbed in any case, so a brick terrace was planned for the centre, keeping a parterre design for the beds on either end. Gordon put down the bricks for the terrace. You will notice that professionals toss down loads of sand, levelling and placing bricks as they go. When they finish, it's level. Firstly, they know how; secondly, as time goes on some of the bricks sink and have to be levelled up again. If you're going to do it yourself, I strongly recommend Gordon's method. He pours on the sand; then, using a straight plank (a hard thing to find these days) plus a carpenter's level, he levels the whole thing. Then he dampens it down thoroughly and waits. The next weekend he levels agains and dampens again, adding sand in the hollows. He keeps on doing this until family and friends are all scream-ing, 'When is he going to lay the bricks?' By the time we are all thoroughly frustrated, the sand is packed hard and smooth as concrete. Then, kneeling on a sheet of plywood, he lays the bricks. Our terrace is ten years old and not a brick has ever had to be re-levelled. All that dampening gave us a bonus: a soft green moss has volunteered in the interstices of the bricks so that it looks old and relaxed. I have to be honest and say that, in its first years, we weeded between the bricks with a vegetable knife to the state of exhaustion. Some people lay plastic under-neath and say it stops the weeds. Walter says it doesn't. They just plant their little irritating selves in the sand you've brushed on between the cracks once the bricks are laid. I should think plastic would keep the patio from draining, but everyone has to make his own decision on this. Personally, I am enamoured of my moss.

Once lattice fence and patio were in, I had only a three-foot strip of earth against the fence. It is simply amazing what can be tucked into three feet. A dozen Festiva Maxima peonies go down the middle of the long side, planted in rich earth. Tucked between and behind, hard against the fence, are climbing roses, New Dawn and Coral Dawn. The front is edged with coral bells (heuchera). As if that weren't enough, Walter squeezed in ten groups of Perry Como tulips and I tried to add clematis between the roses, hoping they would intertwine. It has all been thinned out just a little, because by the third year the mice had eaten the tulips and, try as I will, and replant as I will, only one clematis will grow and that very stingily. But the peonies, the climbing roses and the heuchera thrive, and now that Miranda has eaten most of the mice, I think I'll try Perry Comos again. They are a pale, true pink with a thin line of blue inside as they open. And they are going in deep, deep, planted on sand, with myosotis (forget-me-not) seed sprinkled between.

The so-called parterre beds at either end are planted almost alike. A circular bed, surrounded by a narrow limestone path, leaves a large semi-circular bed against the fence, which swings into a narrow strip beside the flagstone path. It is all outlined in the same old red brick as the terrace, and heuchera, hyssop and sage bushes are planted in matching places at either end. But the rest—basil, garlic chives, French tarragon, lemon balm and whatever else—are tucked in where they're happy, mingling with delphiniums and flowers of all sorts. I redesign every spring and am still not happy with it. The circles at first had been massed with Pink Cascade petunias, which looked divine until August. After an experiment of Sweetheart strawberries as an edging, centre filled with tall perennial geraniums (most untidy), I succumbed and planted white impatiens. Their cool green and white sets off all the colours in the surrounding borders. Sometimes the easy way is the best way.

If you have a herb garden everyone thinks you will be filled with the lore of herbs, and questions are asked. My daughter simply wouldn't believe I didn't know and toured me firmly around doing a 'What's this and what's it for?'

The basil, French tarragon and chives are easy enough. You eat them in salads or on steak. The sage goes into stuffings and makes you wise. But there is one that 'maketh a man merrie.' That must be borage, because it 'driveth away melancholy'. Elizabeth wanted to know whether it really worked, but the only time a friend chopped it into a salad, the men were already merrie enough. It couldn't be called a pure experiment.

The whole subject is complicated, possibly doubtful, and I am just not up on it. For instance, you don't always eat herbs. You can make a poultice, or if you are going bald or losing your memory, you can make a wreath and wear it on your head. Or place a leaf in your shoe. That must be for gout. There is one plant for easing your husband onto a diet: if you place a leaf of basil under his plate, it puts him off his dinner. The best book I have on the subject is Rosetta E. Clarkson's *Herbs and Savory Seeds*. It is not only very informative but enchanting and amusing as well.

Whether you know what they're for or not, tuck herbs into your vegetable and flower gardens. Most of them are well-loved by the other plants and you will love them too when, on a hot day, they perfume the air around you.

Roses on the South Terrace

Now I wish I could open an arched wooden door and lead you out to the amazing view at the back, but we shall just have to be satisfied with stepping through the opening in the hedge. That's right, that needle on the horizon is the CN Tower. If you glance to the left you'll see where Walter stood one day and put Gordon into a panic by saying, 'I'd like to nip the toe off that hill.' At that time the wrist and hand of the long arm of the ridge drifted all across the lawn. Walter skimmed it off, tapered the ridge back, and now we have a back lawn. This left the great part of the ridge bare, and that's why we have the shrub border there. For a time we thought we could get away with it, but, like the perennial border, it looked 'stuck on'. So we have added native shrubs over the entire ridge. 'If you're going to do something, do it' is my motto. It's still not balanced, too thin up there, too thick down here, and needs replanting. Once it's all in bloom, I think I'll do a Victoria Sackville-West and cut flowering branches, then pop them in here and there to see where they look best. If I had one kind of stake for lilac, another for wiegelia and so on, I could drive them in the ground where I want the holes dug. We could fill the holes with all that wonderful topsoil we're going to make, and then replant. Walter's boys move shrubs the way I move geraniums.

When you're planting or transplanting, get all the goodies in below while you can, and fill the hole with water before the plant goes in. I do this even with annuals, using a watering can to fill the hole before I pop the plant in. Then they take right off with no wilting. My Mama taught me that one.

Sorry. I brought you out here to see the roses. To me, they're not all that marvellous; I still have memories of the blooms in the first garden. The Fairy, that flossy pink hedge at the far edge of the terrace and topping the retaining wall, is no trouble at all. These roses are never earthed up, are pruned once, when they're through carrying on like that, and, all in all, are highly satisfactory. So why do I find that dull? Too easy?

Here, going down the west side of the terrace, are the roses I longed for, the hybrid teas. They are planted in good topsoil, which goes down the full depth of the retaining wall. They are backed by a charming little hedge of yew, rarely pruned, and fronted by another charming little hedge of box, kept to a trim, sharp edge. They have drip irrigation, receive quantities of liquid sheep manure and bone meal and are further cosseted with bark mulch. They have no aphids, as you can see, and the black spot is almost eradicated. So why? Why aren't they the roses of the first garden?

I can tell you one thing. I purchased these in big pots. I never plant anything at all with a pot. Pots do *not* rot. When I tipped the roses gently out, the gritty stuff they were planted in fell away, and there were three prongs no longer than my fingers and not a hair root to be seen. They're not producing real bloom because they're desperately trying to build roots.

I asked the head of a large and very good nursery about this and he told me the sad tale. Where once there were ten rose growers in Ontario there are now only two. They mass-produce and, because space is a problem, each cultivar is pruned ruthlessly top and bottom, covered with paraffin and machine-packed. They are then stacked into warehouses and eventually into monstrous trucks and delivered about the country. All part of the same pattern: Big Business, battery hens, cows that never leave the stall, butter stored for years, apples that taste like mush.

I am going to search for a little rose nursery just as I searched for and found little groceries and little fruit stores.

The Wild Garden

If we sit here on the terrace and look down to the poolhouse you can see a planting facing us on the north side. It's mostly ferns and day lilies showing at this time of year. You see, I thought that as the years mounted up I might not be able to wander through the woods to see the hepatica bank above the spring or the trilliums on the high ridge, so I brought a few out where they would be easy to visit. We used cart-loads of their own acid, leaf-mouldy soil first and built up the bed with that. I don't know why I thought wild plants would be delicate or difficult. They're built to last, and if you give them what they want they're marvellously grateful, moving right in and bringing all their relatives. Wild columbine and jack-in-the-pulpit are there under the white birch and pine that shade them. Violets too, but they have no scent and I long for the violets I used to buy in England. I was there when I was young, starving romantically in a garret. Nothing romantic about it, I promise you, just uncomfortable. But one morning a week I would be wakened by a voice a way off, a glorious mezzo singing, 'Who Will Buy?' That's right: the same song you heard in *Oliver*, only she sang, 'Who will buy my bloomin' violets? They're a bunch a penny.' Actually, they were sixpence, but you can't sing that. I would be dressed and down in the street in time to exchange my sixpence for a bunch of deep, dark blooms from her banked-up wooden cart. How I would love to bury my face in those again. Or grow them in the garden.

Time for tea now.

Weather, Wind and Water

We had seen a fair sample of one kind of weather the day we first viewed our property: gale-force winds and snow mixed with ice. But we are rich in weather and have all the other kinds as well. In the country the weather is very much present, smack outside the door, unfiltered by other houses or tall buildings. At times we have our own personal weather. I have driven out in thick snow and at the foot of the driveway found myself in the sun, under clear skies. Puzzled by this, I got out of the car where I could have a clear view, and there was a round curtain of snow falling silently on our twenty acres alone. I felt like Joe BTFLSK. In the summer, praying for rain, I have watched the cloud approach, turn left, meander across the fields, and finally release its burden on someone else's fields, leaving ours still dry as a bone.

Forecasts are of only general help. I was given a book showing how I could do my own forecast by learning the shapes of clouds but, what with one thing and another, never got down to studying it. But now I know. And I don't know how I know. If you spend a great deal of time outdoors you can smell the rain coming, or snow; you can feel it and tell by the colour of the sky. People hereabouts 'call' for the weather. 'They're calling for four feet of snow,' the neighbours say. I don't know who 'they' are; I do know they keep calling for a lot of stuff we could do without. 'They' are calling for a dry spell when the rest of us are crying for a wet spell. But we pay attention, because all you can do about the weather is prepare for it.

Before you buy plants, study your Zone Maps and decide where you are. These maps are in most nursery catalogues and you can receive advice on the problem from knowledgeable salespeople. We are in Zone 4. How I should love to have the holly that grows in B.C., *Rosa wichuraiana*, as groundcover on the south bank, or a fringe tree, but the wind, cranky and cold, says, 'You can't have it; and that's that.' We started, on the advice of local nurseries, to grow what would survive: pine, Austrian pine, mugho pine, savin juniper and viburnum, which takes to the sweet soil and the weather as if born to it. In particular, *Viburnum nana*, a dwarf hedge, planted none too carefully between the gravel of the driveway and the front stone court, prospered from the first, and, though we weren't supposed to, we at last pruned to control its exuberance. Then we decided to gamble a little in the third year and planted Brown's yews (Zones 5 to 9) at the two north corners of the house. They'll die, the nursery told us, but they are thick and luxuriant to the point where one will have to be moved. Other plantings were bewildering. One Russian olive (2b to 9) marches on and the other is in sad retreat.

For deciduous trees we stayed as closely as available stock would allow to what was already in the woods surrounding us, chiefly sugar maple—a highly rewarding tree. This was not only for shade but to achieve a blend with the native surroundings. The Austrian pines now carry the eye on and up the ridge to other pines growing naturally on the hill, tying it all together. At first I resisted evergreens, saying that everything would be buried under snow, but now on a bleak winter day it is cheering to see the great fans of spruce bending to the ground under thick puffs of white. Should a brilliant red cardinal perch there, all is rejoicing.

Close to the house we become less craggy and plant finer, more civilized species; two serviceberry (*Amelanchier canadensis*) accent the steps to the pool and a locust shades the terrace.

In the shrub border, among hardy mock orange (*Philadelphus virginalis*) and honeysuckle, we planted French hybrid lilac. The 'ilac is a mistake in that place. It does need rich loam, and a new home is to be prepared. On the other hand, common lilac, which started here at six inches, has taken to the soil and is beginning to stand tall behind a low ridge to the south. There are twenty-five in a long straggly grouping and each year they will grow taller and more floriferous, drenching us all with scent. All these are tough and can take snow, wind, cold and rain. You do have to experiment to find what will feel at home in your planting zone.

Our rain is special, of course. In other climates you may get a soft rain, gentle and misty. On rare occasions I have seen that here, but in the main, someone takes a long, sharp knife and slits the rain clouds like a barrage balloon and down comes the whole lot. Our first spring here, my children would look up and smile when I called, 'Rain!' Now they, too, run like crazy for the air-raid shelters. It won't hurt you, but it certainly drenches you. Then it all goes away and there'll be no more for weeks and weeks and we have a drought.

Finding perennials that can bear up to all this is a problem. Delphiniums suffer most, and some have been moved to a corner of the lattice fence. Here they are sheltered from the north wind and the south wind blows them flat against the fence, which continues to support them. After a bad rain (how can a rain be bad?) I go out at once and gently shake their heads and those of the peonies to release their burden of water.

Now, that little corner of the lattice fence is what is called a mini-climate. With trees, shrubs, hedges and fences, even a corner of the house, you can create these mini-climates, less riotous with wind and rain, warmer in spring and fall. A little detective work will probably reveal similar small pockets in your own garden.

A friend gave me one of my most precious plants, the Christmas rose (*Helleborus niger*). In most climates this blooms through the snow in February, likes partial shade and should be tucked in against a warm wall. I had the place, by the kitchen door, but the ground was frozen solid and so was the plant, which my friend had cut out as a solid block of ice. So I plugged the electric kettle in and poured boiling water out the door until I had a soft, warm mush, popped the hellebore into that, watered it every day and held its hand for weeks. The following March its buds were thick and curled into the ground. Just as they were about to open, all was buried under two feet of snow.

Undaunted, I ordered ten more from my nice Mr. Keith, keeping in mind that plants like company and trying to devise a way to keep heavy snow at bay. Today it is the twenty-fourth of April, the temperature is 70°F, and the new plants are in full and lovely bloom! The original is just putting out new leaves. I went back to the books and found that my new plants are *Helleborus niger* right enough, but probably of a variety called Chalice, which blooms later. They did have a light powdering of snow last week just to make them look like their photographs. There is a Lenten rose (pink), and endless varieties of the Christmas rose, so that choosing the right cultivar for your mini-climate should present no difficulty. I feel an itch to collect the hellebores if ever I 'collect' anything. If you want them for the table, dip their stems in boiling water first, then plunge into very cold. Don't take their leaves. Helen Van Pelt Wilson says they look enchanting with hemlock, but any dark green will do.

The perennial border stands out in the open in full sun to the north of the house. Wind runs up the tunnel of the driveway, banks left to run down the hill and on its way gives the perennials the full treatment. The idea of a wall or hedge was discarded because it would look both heavy and awkward from the entrance, and now we have planted rugosas to stand on guard.

For a few hundred years the English, particularly, have used the high brick wall and the tall yew hedge to protect their plantings, creating one enchanting outdoor room after another. The high brick wall with arched wooden door stays forever in the memory of anyone who read *The Secret Garden*, and I think we all long to have a walled garden. But apart from the astronomical cost there are the problems of humidity and the size and shape of the property. On the American continent we begin to see an adaptation of the idea in the long narrow plots behind townhouses, and very pretty some of them are. You will note, though, that the fences are all designed to admit a breeze.

My 'secret garden', surrounded by a lattice fence, is very public, as it leads to the garage, the kitchen door and the back terrace. I find I still look about me and wonder how I could contrive an enclosed garden on all these rolling hills. Who would trim all the hedges? Ours does achieve one thing, however: it gives us a protected place from drying winds and hot sun and provides seclusion for breakfast on a bright summer morning. Something of the sort is almost a must for any country garden.

The last exercise in protection comes in the late fall. Now the tender plants are mulched with leaves, compost or straw, according to what suits. In our garden so much is hardy that only the roses receive particular care. Pruning as little as possible, I cover them up to twelve inches with tipis of soil. By now, convinced that the wind does more damage than the cold, I also purchase packets of burlap; it comes in a long twenty-five-foot strip. The burlap is cut in sections, and each rose is individually wrapped and tied after earthing up. This gives a good head start in spring.

An *urgent* word of caution if you use burlap: one winter a mouse took up residence inside the burlap, chewed the threads into a fluffy ball for a nest, then whiled away the dull days of February gnawing the green off the canes right down to the earth line. The plant was a Coral Dawn Climber, which recovered quickly, but after that incident I spray both roses and burlap with SKOOT.

The climbers are released from the trellis fence where they grow behind the peony hedge; then they are tied in a bunch and wrapped (almost double-wrapped) in burlap; the whole bundle is then tied firmly to the fence. This is easier on the plant and easier on me than the practice of bending them down and burying them. In the spring I find the canes still green to the top of the burlap. This is the last chore in the process of putting the garden to bed, and then I know all the treasures are safely tucked in.

In milder climates this may not be necessary. If you have inherited your grandmother's roses you can write me a firm letter stating that these are never protected, bloom happily in the snow, and what am I going on about? What I am going on about is the modern, grafted, hybrid tea rose. Otto Pallek of Carl Pallek & Son very kindly answered all my questions on the subject. Their nursery is at Niagara-on-the-Lake where the climate is milder and the season longer than one would find farther north. They *still* earth up those acres of roses to protect the roots from the disturbance of freeze and thaw; no burlap, of course, which would be an impossible chore with so large an operation. They spray with Benomyl but alternate with other fungicides and insecticides, as diseases will build up an immunity to a spray just as the insects will.

Standing there in mid-July, knee-deep in rows and rows of exuberant bloom, I was sure they must use a chemical booster of some sort but was assured they use only well-rotted manure. However, Mr. Pallek recommends treated weed-free manure for the home gardener, as natural manure harbours disease as well as weeds.

You will find the Pallek nursery's address in Sources. For mild climates they deliver in the fall, but if your ground is frozen by November they recommend spring delivery. Best of all, each plant will arrive with a twelve-inch fibrous root.

Now we come to the subject of water. It turned out to be as big a problem in the garden as it did in and out of the house—either torrential rain or none at all. And, if you remember, we have but a thousand gallons of water a day for the garden and for us. Some days the garden comes first. I have no patience with plastic hoses and purchased four hundred feet of good rubber hose in hundred-foot lengths. It's heavy. Now the trees and shrubs stand on their own feet, but when they were first planted water was essential if we were not to lose them all. I joined all the hoses together and hauled from tree to shrub to tree. Four hundred feet was not long enough, and for the far trees I found myself filling watering cans and trudging over the hills. Besides Walter's planting, the local conservation authority had planted two hundred six-foot whips of maple, basswood and locust, plus shrubs and common lilac. Everything was thirsty. In the two seasons when this was on, I perfected my own Indian Rain Dance, all to no avail. But at last they could make it on their own, and I had only the vegetable garden, the perennial border, the rose beds, the side garden, the plantings by the steps, and the two lawns to worry about.

We owned absolutely every type of watering device that was ever invented: tall ones in the vegetable garden, a busy little engine that ran around the lawns, forever turning itself upside down, and large fan types that watered the air and came down slosh on the flowers. Hours were spent shifting these devices about, so I resorted to soaker hoses and soaker tapes, which worked until they sprang a leak. Then I heard about the irrigation system perfected by the Israelis. It was a special form of PVC pipe that could be bent and twisted without breaking and could be put together in all manner of shapes. The first irrigation firm I called had it. They insisted I buy a small kit first, install it myself, and see if I liked it. Gordon installed it: shoving the pipe into the drippers takes muscle. (You can soften the pipe up by dipping it into hot water.) It didn't matter whether I liked it—the roses were mad about it: no water on their leaves, all they wanted at their roots, and while they were being watered we could sit on the terrace without being sprayed.

The following spring this system was run through the perennials (four or five lines), through the side garden, even to the tiny circles that stand alone, and, from a pipe running underground, a full system was put into the vegetable garden. This system uses 70 percent less water than sprinklers but we put in four separate systems, only one to be on at a time. Testing has now shown that we can turn them all on at once. Before tossing the golf clubs into the car, we open all four faucets; then we come back four hours later and close the faucets. They're not on every day, of course. For winter, only the rose system is lifted, because of earthing them up. In the main, the lines stay out all winter, though the installers blow them clear before freezing. If we had a better water supply I would install sprayers in the two lawns as well, though I have heard these can choke up with earth. You will have gathered that I am recommending this system. Now we play golf three times a week instead of once every three. We're no better, but we play more.

If you are to enjoy your garden you can't be a slave to it, so gradually add the best labour-saving devices you can afford.

NOTES FOR THE NOVICE

Shopping Guide

Once upon a time I bought a car because it was a pretty colour. Not until I was behind the wheel did I discover that this magnificent machine took off like a jet and cruised at 90 mph. On ice, this proved to be impractical. The wise person, when purchasing a car, will visit all the showrooms, collect and study all the brochures, mull over the pros and cons of four-wheel drive, front-wheel drive, four-door, two-door, peer into the engine and, at the very least, kick the tires. In the end, he asks the man who owns one. *How does it perform*? That is the key question.

And that is the key question when it comes to the choosing of trees, shrubs and other large investments for the garden. These will be with you long after you have parted with your car. Give their purchase the same deep thought, study and enquiry and ask the man who owns one. This is what the catalogues mean when they warn, 'Buy the right plant for the right place.'

TREES

Trees work for a living. Ask yourself first what you want the tree to do. It can screen out dust, deflect the wind, provide deep shade or dappled shade, modify the climate, provide privacy, year round or just in summer. It can add stature, even grandeur, to a property or simply lend grace and charm. It can raise the water table. A full-grown tree pumps up forty gallons of water per day and transpires this moisture into the air. However, it can be a pest, dripping debris all summer long, snaking its roots into the flower beds or, worse, the underground service trenches. It can emit poison into the earth around, allowing nothing else to grow.

How do you choose? There are restrictions on your choice,

which will make life simpler. What will grow to full health in your climate, your immediate growth zone and your type of soil? The local nurseries, and a stroll through your neighbourhood, will answer these questions. And here is your chance to enquire about its bad habits, if any.

Size is the next criterion. We are often advised to plant small trees on small properties, but there are towns all over Canada and the U.S. where our forefathers planted maple, elm and other sixty-foot trees along the boulevards. High-pruned, they leaf out above the rooftops to create a canopy of shade for the dog-days of summer. They are in the right place.

That is the next thing to think of: place. You will see willows planted around a country pond, a thousand feet from the house, a joy to all. In the front yard of a one-storey cottage they are both ludicrous and a nuisance. A blue spruce planted a good fifty feet from the house and spreading its skirts wide on a green lawn is in the right place, but planted against the living-room window, and many are, it leads to gloom within and without. A big tree can be the right plant only if you put it in the right place.

Does it belong? Here is another reason for studying what surrounds you. On a city street, if you pick up and repeat or accent what is already there, the entire area becomes a part of your garden. In the country we found that the most successful plantings were those that repeated the maple, pine, ash and hemlock that surrounded us.

A rose may be a rose, but a tree is forever, the joy of your garden or the bane of your existence, so take your time, improve your soil, put in grass and think it all through. You have time. As they say out here if I tap an impatient foot, 'What's the hurry? You have all your life, Mrs. Keeble.'

ORNAMENTAL TREES AND SHRUBS

For us, the multi-trunked silver maples, white birch and serviceberry (*Amelanchier canadensis*) are ornamental trees, accents for a bed of flowers below, but on a city property any one of them could well be the principal tree of the garden. With the advent of the mechanical tree planter—the monster that lifts an immense cone out of the earth and then, in one move, pops in the tree—gardeners hereabouts have been planting trees like petunias, with horrendous results. Unless you are planning a copse of trees, or a spinney, I again urge caution. Treat each tree as the perfect jewel, to be perfectly placed.

For flowering trees and shrubs, think COLOUR. This comes first—before size, shape or fragrance. They bloom in spring and, if you are not to have your teeth on edge, they must enhance the scarlets and yellows of tulips. Many of the rose or pink tulips are too delicate to hold their own, though 'Perry Como' is a joy from bud to petal fall. To save myself trouble, I have chosen the white-blooming Red Jade crabapple, which arches its branches out in a parasol shape over the flower border. Hand-pick this type of shrub, scouting through the nurseries until you can put your hand on the exact tree and say, '*That one*!' (It took me two years to find it, and out of fifteen only that one was right.) If you settle for the rose- or wine-flowering shrubs, avoid the cerise and red tulips; some yellows might be possible.

The serviceberry will give you white bloom in spring and a singing scarlet in autumn. The colour of shrubs in the fall must be considered as well. Forsythia will hold its golden leaves until November. Purpleleaf sandcherry is a deep burgundy, Russian olive is the silver of sage and the crabapples glow with tiny scarlet fruit. You can cool these off with the greens of lilac and other shrubs and blend all with the background of trees turning to red and gold.

Size, of course, does matter, particularly width, so check the labels and give them breathing space.

LOW EVERGREENS

Will they grow old gracefully? Because I like my evergreens green, soft and easy to control, I lean towards yew, but pine and juniper—especially the low, spreading junipers—can be lovely if you allow for their full width, and they are not the type to turn scraggy and brown. Less can look like more if you set them well apart on pebble mulch or deep brown bark; allow the long branches to fan out over stone paving. They have a certain formality and are ideal for the city garden.

GROUNDCOVERS

Are they well-mannered? This is absolutely the first thing to ask. I have heard unkind words with regard to goutweed, crown vetch and linum. Cotoneaster was perfect on a wide, steep bank and anathema in the shrub border. Ajuga and the delicate *Vinca minor* are beautifully behaved, as is thyme. Ivy? Maybe yes, maybe no. Ask the lady who grows it in your neighbourhood.

Where Do You Learn All This?

Your neighbours' gardens and your closest botanical gardens are the best sources of information. Here you can see the real thing in full growth and at all seasons, in combination with other trees and shrubs. If the staff are not busy, you can ask questions.

Some wholesale gardens will let you look and others won't. Carl Pallek, right by Niagara-on-the-Lake, allowed us into his fields to see roses, labelled and in full bloom. (Pallek's ships from coast to coast.) Almost next door is Mori Gardens, which grows truly dwarfed pine, juniper, spruce and yew.

Nursery catalogues often have good information, as do magazine articles. You will have to turn to books as well. These are to buy or to borrow, to read for pleasure or for reference: *Native Trees of Canada*, by R.C. Hosie, includes coniferous and deciduous trees native to both Canada and the U.S.; easy identification by photographs. *The Time-Life Encyclopedia of Gardening* has photographs and coloured drawings; text informative on where and how to plant; individual volumes for shrubs, evergreens, etc. *Manual of Cultivated Plants* by Liberty H. Bailey: formidable at first glance, but once you find your way in it, you will be able to identify everything and anything. You will also learn the Latin names. To pursue this further, read his *How*

Plants Get Their Names. These are not pretty picture books: they are tomes. If you wish to pronounce the Latin properly, try to lay hands on the *New Pronouncing Dictionary of Plant Names*. (Publication details for all these can be found on page 218.) Two excellent magazines, full of new information, are *Harrowsmith* and *Organic Gardening*.

Your best source of good books will be the library of a good horticultural garden. For instance, the Civic Garden Centre at Edwards Gardens in Don Mills has a wide choice. Never, never choose a book by its cover. Look up a plant in the index, then turn to the page indicated and see if it really does tell you what you want to know. Browse through the book as well as the store.

Facts aren't everything, however, and there are many authors (Victoria Sackville-West, Gertrude Jekyll, Thalassa Cruso, Helen Van Pelt Wilson) who are simply a joy to read for themselves, all apart from the information. When it comes to gardening, you can never know too much.

Keeping Track

I hope that Notes for the Novice will inspire you to keep your own notes. If so, buy a book calendar with a full page for each date. For example:

November 9

1985 (30°) Bulb order arrived. 2 inches of snow! Waiting for thaw to plant.

1986 (30°) Rain and sleet. Bulbs here. Waiting for weather to clear.

1987 (28°) Snow. Finished planting bulbs Oct. 31. Garden closed.

If you glance back quickly to the same day a year ago, you will soon learn when to pick up your bulbs—winter comes early every year. Similarly, in spring you can avoid such entries as 'Surprised by late frost, tomato plants frozen.' Spring comes late every year.

Keep a separate notebook on flowers or shrubs with photos or cut-out pictures to illustrate each page. Then, as you accumulate information from books, lectures or your own experience, you will have it under its proper heading and all in one place for reference.

Both notebooks will prove very useful if you remember two things:

1. Make the entry, and
2. Go back and read it.

Helps and Helpers

If a man has a city garden, he will be content with a spade, a fork, a rake and a good power mower. He might just add a sprayer. But put him on five acres in the country and the first thing he wants is a tractor, the bigger the better. Bright red. The only tractor that will handle the grass, the snow and the hills out here now costs $50,000, plus attachments. The only way to get the value out of that is to have a hundred acres and hire yourself out to clear snow and plough fields. Then you need a barn to store it.

What most of us do is buy a 16 h.p. and ride that around merrily for a while, wearing a straw hat, then phone the nearest farmer and hire him to do the job. Meanwhile, you have to build something to store your own small tractor. We attached a third garage to the two we had, to be the garden shed. We should have built a barn. The shed now contains:

FLOOR SPACE TO HOLD: one tractor with mower, one tractor cart, two wheelbarrows (one large and one small), one tiller, one power reel mower, one power rotary mower.

SHELVES TO HOLD: rope, sprinklers, 400 feet of garden hose, watering cans, electric extension cords, barbeque, seeds, fertilizers, axe, tree stakes, plant stakes, etc.

HOOKS TO HOLD: three shovels, two garden rakes, one stone rake, two forks (long and short), apple picker, back sprayer, two hand sprayers, dust gun, two lawn edgers, whipper-snippers (two because one doesn't work), snow shovels, ice chippers, tractor chains, six bushel baskets and five types weeding hoes.

A SIX-QUART BASKET TO HOLD: trowel, cultivator, fork, two pair secateurs, scissors, twine, tape measure, small stakes, hand weeder, etc. etc. (All mine! Don't touch! Put it back!)

There is not enough room here to list it all, and there is not enough room in the shed to store it all. For a while the firewood was in there too, but now it is out under its own shelter. Wood dries best in the open in any case.

Larry and Nancy R. inherited Harold's old tractor when Harold and Dot moved to New York; it just came along with the house. Harold had inherited it from the Campbells who, for all I know, had inherited it from the McBrides in 1890. This is a glorious machine. Larry and his son-in-law spend happy hours (and I mean hours) cleaning its gaskets and repairing its belts. At dusk, at last, they emerge, with triumphant roars of machine and men, to rock and waver about the fields. Something of similar character might be unearthed at a farm auction. That failing, a new tractor can be depended on to blow its carburetor, drop a pin or just run out of gas. Hours of puttering about come along with the guarantee.

You do have to have one. A tractor hauls. It hauls earth, leaves, manure, wood in its little cart—in small quantities, mind, but if you don't have it you'll be doing all that hauling with a wheelbarrow. Hire the big machine for the big jobs or where steep hills are involved. The small one can tip over.

I have only one piece of advice on garden equipment. All the way down from the tractor through the spade to your secateurs, buy the absolute best, the top of the line. Garden equipment takes a beating and there's nothing more useless than secateurs that won't cut and edgers that won't edge. Even worse is not being able to find the tool you want. Be sure you build a shed or small barn that's big enough. (It won't be.) Have a definite place for everything and hang up signs. CLEAN IT OFF. PUT IT BACK. (They won't.)

The one thing we didn't need was the reel mower. It is superb and expensive, and it catches all the clippings, but unless you have a lawn like broadloom, and flat as a billiard table, it just bounces about. Now I wonder if we need mowers at all.

We have been fortunate in the help we have, but we live in the country, and, as one old grandfather said, 'Our boys know what it is to be told what to do.' Not all the boys are this disciplined, but other types won't even ask for the job.

The boys who have shown up also know what it is to work. At first we made the mistake of working alongside. Young Norman was only twelve, but at noon Gordon said, 'If we try to keep up with that kid, we'll both have a stroke.' We quit and Norman carried on like a young dynamo, weeds falling over dead at his approach. He stayed two years, but it couldn't last. He was snaffled off by a very canny businessman who is grooming him to be president of the company.

Serendipity takes over around here, I've noticed, and when Norman went on to a bright future, a man with a strong back left a note in our mailbox. That was Rudy. Rudy built the vegetable garden into its present form, dug big holes and cleaned the windows or the basement; but he, too, found a better job.

The main difficulty with the man who came once a week was that it rained on the only day he was available. Then serendipity took over again. About five one evening, I answered the door to an old friend. I had him in by the fire by the time Gordon came home, and the three of us reminisced about old times. Not until he was at his car and about to leave did he look around and say, 'This is one big garden! Do you ever need help with it?' His son Waldo was in the garden maintenance business.

When I called and got the prices, my heart sank. It would cost as much per hour for his team as I paid in a day for one man. But we gave it a try.

At eight in the morning I was startled to hear the roaring of machines. Flying from window to window, I saw three boys with three big mowers, riding them or walking them at a fast canter, and a girl working her way down the staircase, cutting the grass platforms between the steps. The long cuttings in the rough grass were being blown away with a hand-held blower. Someone was edging the flower beds like lightning. In less than an hour, they were loading up and driving away. ''It's all at three and a half inches—that OK?' I nodded and they were gone.

They cost less. They use their own machines and their own gas. If it rains they come another day. They come only when the grass needs cutting, and they decide about that. They roll it with a steam-roller. They feed it and they keep every blade at the same height. One call at the beginning of the season and a cheque at the end of each month is all I have to do. This sort of outfit can usually do special jobs, pruning or hedge-trimming, when you need them. And how does all this help you when you don't live here? Chances are, there's a firm like this where you live. Phone around and ask for references. Try them once and you may solve the boring task of lawn maintenance. Flowers can be fun. Grass isn't.

About once a month the weeds get ahead of me, and Sue comes to weed and tidy up. She came originally to help Rick close the pool, and I was pulling the dead leaves away from the day lilies. They didn't want to let go, but cold weather was coming fast and I didn't want to leave mats of dead leaves around them. 'Stubborn, aren't they?' said Sue, and her hand came down and gave them an expert tweak. This was no helper—this was a gardener. We made a deal right then.

The first time she came was a hot day in spring. She was wearing short shorts and a sleeveless top. I looked at her lovely long bare legs and thought of all the prickly roses she was about to prune and the hard bricks she would be kneeling on, but Sue said she would be just fine. No—no leather gloves, thanks. Her cotton work gloves were what she was used to. At the end of four hours she had expertly pruned a long hedge of that scratchy, brambly rose, the Fairy, weeded two brick terraces, the stone walk and the stone terrace, and scuffle-hoed the gravel of the service yard. Then she had spread bone meal on ten long vegetable beds and reshaped them so that they looked as if they'd been popped out of a giant muffin pan. When she had cleaned off the tools and put them back, I went out to pay her and couldn't believe my eyes. She was just as band-box fresh as when she arrived.

I have been trying to figure it out ever since. I think I have it but can't be sure I can explain it. When I go out to weed, I'm thinking 'five hundred weeds' and when I'm having at the first one, I'm thinking about the other four hundred and ninety-nine, swivelling around to get that one over there and swiv-elling back to get another, on my knees, determined to have the whole lot out before lunch time.

Sue focusses quietly on one weed. She is in the right position, has the right tool, winkles it out and coolly places it in the weed basket. And so, from weed to weed, from task to task, unhur-rying, enjoying it, not thinking about time. That's Zen, isn't it? I must ask David; he'll know. At any rate, try to be a Sue and not a me.

If you think you are more like me and need all the help you can get, there is one other list of equipment:

GARDENING GLOVES: I don't mean those silly cotton things. I have three pairs of washable heavy leather gloves. You can get them in women's sizes where they sell riding togs. When you're pruning roses and other prickly growths, they're a godsend.

SHOES: Leather for protection with good support, waterproof, and with lots of room for your toes to spread when you squat down. You'll need two, possibly three, pair. They have to be washable, too.

SLACKS AND TOPS: We all start with jeans and then discover that we can't bend over. I like jogging or exercise outfits that are stretchy and cover me from neck to ankle and down to wrists. They breathe and will flip into washer and dryer. The dirt is on them, not me, and I don't end up with a farmer's tan. For hot, hot weather, look for thin, crinkly Indian cotton.

HATS: I can't help you. A good gardener's hat is as hard to find as a good golfing hat. I think what I want is one of those coolie hats that balance, cool and light, on top of the head, like an umbrella.

A BENCH: You can weed and plant from a firm, non-tippable bench. Knees wide apart, toes turned out, bend forward from the big hinges where legs meet torso (you do not have a hinge below the small of your back). Let your chin drop and rest on your chest. When reaching for a tool beside you sit up and walk yourself around, still seated, then bend again keeping the back straight. Don't lift your chin when reaching—it's straining and twisting that get us into trouble. Try it. You'll be surprised to find how much you can do and how much better you feel when you keep your weight off your knees and feet.

A TIMER: When the bell rings, ready or not, finished or not, *stop*.

LASTLY: A good masseuse, a good podiatrist and a long, wide, deep bathtub with an arsenal of lotions and potions. Take care of yourself. The garden needs you.

Birds, Bees and Other Weirds

Birds

One of the first things you'll do on coming to the country is buy a bird book. I like the *Audubon Society Field Guide*, but look them all over. I also have some of the Bent *Life Histories* Series, on the birds that concern me; he gives their lives in excruciating detail. Colin Harrison's *Field Guide to Nests, Eggs and Nestlings* is interesting. You can get carried away on this subject. You'll need a pair of good binoculars too. Then you'll put up a bird-feeding station close to the house and spend next spring weeding sunflowers out of the rose bed. Try to station it in a tree, set in the grass away from flower beds and near shrubs.

Winter is lovely. That is when the birds bring life to an otherwise bleak and still landscape. Brilliant blue jays, purple finches, scarlet cardinals all hob-nob with the neat little juncos and chickadees. The downy woodpecker swings crazily about, upside down on a suet ball. The mourning doves (and, to my annoyance, someone's matched pairs of pigeons) perambulate with great self-importance on the ground, though nothing is as stately as the big black crows in spring; they look solemn as undertakers. The real joy for us this far north is the snow buntings. They come in flocks of fifty, wheeling in unison, attached by an invisible web. They're white with a thin brown stripe on head and wing. One winter day as the sun was setting, a flock settled all facing one way in the locust tree. The sun changed the brown stripe to gold and there they were, each wearing a thin gold circlet on its head. Enchanted princesses, obviously, straight out of *Giselle*.

Spring comes and the problems start. If ever you wondered where 'bird-brain', 'feather-brain' or 'air-head' came from, you have only to watch a mother bird in action. They keep losing their kids. When they find them, they carry on as if it were the baby's fault. If you put the baby back in the nest, it promptly falls out again and now the mother won't touch it because you did.

I spent a harrowing two days, three years ago, when a swallow built her nest on the barn beam crossing under the roof of the pool-house. Now we couldn't use the pool-house and had to sit out on the deck, well to one side.

From there I watched the proceedings. Four heads with open beaks were visible. Mama flew in and out, stuffing food into the beak on the left. I couldn't believe it. None of that 'one for you and one for you' stuff. The biggest beak and the longest neck got it all.

I remonstrated, 'How about the little fellow on the right?' Perhaps they shifted around, but not while I was watching. However, when the time came for them to fly away, all four wheeled off into the sky.

Two more heads appeared. All this time they'd been underneath, trampled by their siblings and getting nary a bite. They were very small, very weak and scared out of their teeny-tiny wits. Mama didn't feed them. She urged them up until they were teetering on the edge of the nest. Then she nagged and nagged them to fly. They were terrified.

By now I was beside myself and found myself calling a bird a bird-brain. 'Feed them!'

The rest of the story is very sad. The first baby fell to the deck. I attended his funeral. The second managed to get his wings open before he hit the deck and spent two days staggering around, wings outspread, but couldn't take off. I abandoned everything and baby-sat for two days, keeping him out of the pool, but he managed to drown himself at dawn before I was up. And if you think I'm weird, you should hear what some of my friends have gone through. Sometimes I just can't stand birds.

But there are birds and there are birds. A pair of eastern bluebirds ignored our nesting boxes and raised their young deep in a north shrubbery, against all the rules. They are supposed to prefer a box, out in the open, facing south. (Well, they hadn't read the book.) On a lovely summer day the parents stationed themselves about eight feet apart in two apple trees. The two babies then went through a 'Fly to Mummy, now fly to Daddy' routine back and forth, practising landings and take-offs, while four of us sat on the steps, afraid to breathe. It went on for an hour and we will never understand that one. Obviously the babies had flown from the nesting site to the apple tree; so why all the practice? A pair of caring parents.

Just like snowflakes, no two birds are alike. I discovered this when a wood thrush burst into song in the red maple tree. His song filled the garden, the magnificent tone soared to the sky. A Pavarotti of a bird! Praying he would never stop, I stayed to the very end. For the next few days I kept an eye out for him, and at last there he was, in the same tree and almost the same branch. I waited. He sang. It wasn't the same bird. It was the same song, very pretty, but he didn't have the chest, the arch to the beak, the great chambers in his little skull for resonance. And you know, he didn't give a damn? He sang anyway. It seemed only polite to hear him out and, as he threw all his heart and soul into it, I found it difficult to decide which bird I admired more.

Should you think I exaggerate, I have witnesses. Ro and her husband John recently bought and refurbished a beautiful old farmhouse just a mile up the line. It was meant for weekends, but in May they decided to try country living full time. Early one morning, Ro called. Did I have a bird book?

'This bird . . . it sang . . . you've never heard . . . you can't believe . . . '

'Yes, I can. It was a thrush.'

'Its beak was straight and its colour was—oh I couldn't see— if you could have heard . . . '

By now I had my Audubon Field Guide in hand, turned to page 667. 'Ro? Here it is. Now listen carefully. This is what Thoreau had to say. ''Whenever a man hears it he is young, and Nature is in her spring; wherever he hears it, it is a new world and a free country, and the gates of heaven are not shut against him." '

All I could hear was Ro softly breathing.

'That it?'

She managed to say yes, very quietly.

'There you are then. It was a wood thrush,' and I gently replaced the receiver, leaving her to contemplate the wonders of country living, in a garden, in the spring.

Bees

I know I shouldn't get into this. It really is weird, and what is more, I don't understand it. Long ago I settled myself with a book and a cool drink in the Sand Garden, waiting for the train to go by. No sooner settled than a bee dived at my ear, then my nose. I got up and walked about and he followed. I sat again and there he was. Why I should have remembered at that moment that my English grandmother 'told the bees' I don't know. In her part of Shropshire, if there was a birth, death or wedding (and that was just about all the excitement there was) the lady of the house went to the hives and 'told the bees'.

I contemplated the pesky creature in front of me. There was no one around. So I told it, 'No one's been born, died or married that I know of, but here's the family news in brief.' He flew away.

Nancy C. joined me some days later and so did the bee. 'That thing is driving my crazy,' she said. I told her what I had tried and Nancy, an unbeliever if ever there was one, looked at it and said crisply, 'The news hasn't changed since the last time.' It flew away and neither of us cared to comment.

Years and years passed during which I held no further conversations with bees. Then we come to the country garden and more years pass. The Canterbury bells had gone off and had to be cut, so I went out with my flower cutters and couldn't get at them for bees. There's no one around in the country and you can find yourself talking to everything from the cat to the cows, so thoughtlessly I remarked, 'Why can't you move to the borage? You like that,' and, giving up, turned away to find something else to snip. When I turned back they were all on the borage. Three or four, too groggy to move, lingered on, deep in a bell. I cut those down carefully and swathed down the rest, wondering. It doesn't make sense, you see. People who spend their lives in research on bees will tell you that a single bee is not really an individual. The swarm is the individual. Yet talking to one bee had worked too. Do bees have ears? Well, you will agree that it's strange. I will confess that, if I am absolutely sure no one can possibly hear me, I will talk to a bee; so I should no doubt add myself to the list of weirds.

The Racing Charolais

We do not keep animals. But Harold and Dot, who had a large barn and a large field, felt they should really get into the country living style. They started with two horses. That was a lovely interlude. We could see them, manes flying, galloping from here to there in the distant field. But, deciding they wanted something quieter and only the best, they sold the horses and acquired six Charolais cows.

Sunday morning we were at the toast stage when Harold pounded on the kitchen door. Agonized and apologetic, he told us that the cows were loose somewhere on our property and would trample down the garden. Dot ran up and called to me, 'Get a rake!' I got the rake. What was I supposed to do with it? We organized; Harold's daughter Cindy took off north in the jeep, Dot took off in the station wagon, heading west, and Harold and Gordon started down along the fence into the woods.

'You stand on guard,' they said and left me all alone in the morning sunshine. At last I found out what the rake was for. If you set it, prongs down, on the grass and wrap an arm around the handle, it makes a nice thing to lean on while you warm your bones in the sun and munch your toast. Ages passed. Aeons passed. I gazed out at the far fields. A funny-looking red-gold ball was coming out of the woods into Harold's field. There was another. The balls had four legs. The Charolais were back in their own field and there was no one to tell.

The cows circumnavigated our property in this wise every Sunday morning (Cindy's beau was leaving the gate open every Saturday night). Then the inevitable happened; he left our gate open as well. Instead of turning sharp left and coming up our drive, the cows turned sharp right, out through our gate and moved briskly onto the 7th line. They were seen, moving at a fast trot, heading for the Airport Road. Going south, and now very inspirited by the passing cars, they cantered to the flashing light, turned on to the Peel County Road and, when they came to Highway 10, took the home stretch at a full gallop with everyone in hot pursuit. Then they saw a lush green field and dashed in, and the farmer ran to the gate and locked it.

All interested parties gathered in the field. The farmer turned to Harold. 'Those are fine beasts.'

'Yes, they are,' said Harold.

'A little thin.'

'Well, they run a lot.'

After further exchanges, a deal was struck, and the Charolais settled into their new home. 'It was either that or enter them at Woodbine racetrack,' said Harold. Cindy found a new beau.

Miranda

We were urged by one and all to (a) keep chickens, (b) fatten cows, (c) build a pond and buy ducks, but we were content to share in our friends' amazing adventures. We had all the animals we wanted in the woods. They took care of themselves and wandered out to visit when the mood struck them. And we had Miranda. In the early days, she got herself talked about.

'That cat is wearing eye-liner.'

'And bangs. Bangs?'

'Who does she think she is—Marilyn Monroe?'

You may guess she was not all that popular with the ladies, but men would cuddle her up and purr along with her, 'You should just feel this cat's coat.' All of which sounds as though she devoted her time to being ornamental but we knew just how hard she worked for her living. At first there was a slight problem of territory. In the first week she had disappeared overnight and in the morning I went out to the top of the hill, sending a clarion call: Miraaandaaa! This had always brought her lolloping home, but not this time. For the sake of the neighbours, the calling and hallooing had to be spaced out, and after an hour I decided I would have to search along the roads; but just as I got to the top of the driveway I could see coming in at the gate one small, very, very tired cat. She tried to run, gave up, and just lay down on the gravel, so I carried her home. After that, nothing would persuade her to walk out through the gate or into the woods. We were accompanied on all walks around the property, but at the gate or the woods she would sit down firmly and wait for us to come back.

Now, with her own boundaries staked out in her head, she went to work. No mice. Our mice are really voles and some of them are full of fight. Her nose was scratched, her paw bitten, but she battled on to clear the garden of all voles, an impossible task. Suitors came to call, unaware that after her visit to the vet, she just wasn't interested. The fur would fly, and one morning, finding huge tufts of white fur all over the terrace, we realized that Barbara's tom must be walking around in his skin. I phoned to apologize, but Barbara just said, 'Serves him right.' When a neighbour's dog came over the hill, Miranda dropped belly to ground, clawed her way through the grass toward him, the front hissing and spitting like a small steam engine and the caboose twitching with tail swinging back and forth. The dog froze in amazement, then turned and ran. Groundhogs she never figured out. She would drop to the ground and stare. The groundhog would stare. They never got closer than two yards. The staring match would go on and then, as though by mutual agreement, they would both turn and walk away.

But the birds? What were we to do about the birds? We decided the first time she caught one we would have to get her a collar with a bell. I was sunning on the front porch when she came in, tail proudly erect, bringing me a live brown thrasher held lightly in her mouth, for all the world like a retriever. I am ashamed to say I smacked her hard, jumping up and down and yelling, 'No! No birds!' Her mouth opened and the bird flew off unharmed. I sat down again on the porch and Miranda approached, looking more puzzled than offended. She patted my knee with her paw to get attention. I tried to explain, 'Birds? No. Mice? Yes. I'm sorry I hit you, Miranda, but no birds. Birds are out.' Then I came to and realized I was talking to a cat. We looked for and couldn't find a bell that would fit a cat. But as the hunt went on we came to realize we wouldn't need it—she wasn't catching birds. She would chitter at them, watch them closely and switch her tail, then sigh and go off to look for a mouse.

Howard and Bob, who had come to paint the house, explained the whole thing. 'She can talk.' She certainly made a lot of strange noises, but talk? All I knew was that the three of them would sit out in the sun at noon hour, holding long conversations while she ate all the chicken in their sandwiches.

Was she a cat? We weren't all that sure. If she could talk and wouldn't catch birds? She was just Miranda—a little weird.

The Invaders

In the days of the Crusaders people built their homes high on the hills for purposes of defense. When the wars simmered down they abandoned the stone walls, moat, and portcullis to settle in the valleys where the soil was deep and fertile and the house was protected from the weather. If we stand up by our vegetable garden we can see the enemy approach from miles away to the north, east and south, giving us plenty of time to man the ramparts. But on the west and north-west we are out-flanked; the woods march there the full length of our property and extend back, joining other woods, to Highway 9 and east to the town-line.

The guns came. We had heard stories of farmers losing their hats to a bullet as they ploughed and other hair-raising anecdotes, but it wasn't until the first hunting season of our residence here that we gave much credence to them. At first it was a strange bugling sound, later identified as a beagle. This was followed by the crack of a gun. Way off in the distance, we said. That hunter was joined the following weekend by another. When his bullet hit the bitternut hickory in the front yard we began to sit up and take notice. The police said we should post our land. This meant nailing NO TRESPASSING and NO HUNTING signs every fifty feet around the entire twenty acres. We did that. They used the signs for target practice. We developed tremendous lung power and shouted admonitions and warnings, the language getting stronger as time went by. When the police arrived the hunters had departed. I was getting used to bullets flying around my ears, taking on the mental attitude of the mindless driver who thinks he can never be hit.

Then three local lads arrived to repair a crack in the stucco. At the first report of a gun, all three were in the kitchen and shouting into the phone.

'That was no .22! By the front door!' they yelled, and the

police arrived. The hunter had gone, but the local boys were so exercised, the officer got firm with me. 'Call us at the first shot next time. We may have a cruiser near by.'

The next time, Gordon and I were reclining in the sun by the pool. First we heard the beagle. When the gun went off we yelled, and though he could hear us perfectly well, he went on shooting. Only then did it dawn on us that we were dealing with a mental case. Gordon used the phone in the pool-house, then said, 'We have to get out of here.' We went up the steps doubled over, for all the world like something out of *The Guns of Navarone*. Just as we collapsed into the kitchen, another gun started up on the high ridge. The man with the beagle took off; we could hear the dog rapidly fading into the distance. At that moment a cruiser whizzed into our drive, and as the officer stepped out, the man on the ridge fired. Now we had the officer in our kitchen, on the phone and calling out the reserves. He told us that the procedure was to circle the roads looking for a parked car and wait until the hunters come out. The police will go into the woods if they have to, but finding a man in there is dicey.

There was no car and that could mean just one thing: it was a neighbour. We took care of that with a series of polite phone calls: 'If you see a man walking into our woods with a gun, would you mind awfully letting us know, or the police know? The police want him.' One of the calls hit the target, and the man on the ridge never came back. Gordon took care of the man with the beagle by shooting into the ground with our wobbly .22. He, too, departed. Guns made him nervous, I suppose.

The peace of the ensuing autumns was idyllic. The years went by. The house was finished. The basic part of the garden was in. Euphoria at last.

Gordon was cleaning out suckers from the front trees and I was lazily weeding when a mild little man appeared over the hump that leads into the road allowance. All he carried in his hand was a small can of white spray paint. Casually he would squirt at a tree as he walked by. Mildly interested, Gordon asked him what he was doing.

'Marking a trail,' he said. 'This is a road allowance. Public property.' Then he walked rapidly on. Oh well, a few people strolling through now and then wouldn't matter. Might be rather nice.

First they came in threes and fours; then over thirty went through, ten of them with dogs running loose. Next two groups of thirty-five. The neighbour at the foot of our drive was beginning to crack: all these people with dogs were debouching into her front yard. I was fairly twitchy myself. Who were they?

I stopped two nice-looking women and asked. They were the Bruce Trail Association. It was one of these ladies who told me firmly that I had to get it stopped. 'We don't like disturbing other people's privacy. And do you realize the position you are in? Anyone can stand at the top of the ridge out of sight and overlook your entire property. They can see if you leave and know that the house is standing empty. They can see if you're alone in the house.' The ridge she was referring to is the second ridge to the west of the house, heavily wooded, and the place from where our solitary gunman had taken pot-shots into the front yard. I walked up there myself and was amazed to discover that it was possible to see all around the house and every detail of the grounds. That was one danger; the other was for the hikers themselves. The trail led through what we called a bog but was in reality quicksand, and overhead, in the tall trees, heavy branches broken off by the wind lay lightly balanced in the leaves. Any disturbance could bring one crashing down.

And now school classes were coming through, with their dogs and one solitary teacher, shouting and calling, having a lovely time. A bus would meet them at the foot of our drive and hand out their lunches. My neighbour would call to say she had counted ninety-eight children and eleven dogs, half of them in her garden, and that the Coke tins and lunch bags were all over the road. She thought we had to do something. I thought so too. But what?

The road allowance crossed one hundred feet from our front door, just behind the fence, so that the house was filled all day with the shouts of the passing throngs. The General Public had followed on the heels of the Bruce Trail members. Maps had been handed out to sport stores in Toronto and all local schools notified. One gentleman called me over to the fence to tell me that it was a terrible walk, 'all thick bush, slimy underfoot and nothing to see.' I looked down at his large hiking boots. Beneath the soles were wood violet, bloodroot, trout lily and a single jack-in-the-pulpit. He tramped off, making the trail slimier than ever with dead plants. General Public has very large feet, too many feet, and careless hands that tear at branches for support. Young saplings had been cut or torn down to clear the trail. I wondered, too, if they were all non-smokers. All it would take was one match.

Letters went out in all directions. The replies were polite, sympathetic and of no help. We had known from the beginning that the road allowance would be a problem and had tried, in concert with our neighbours Bruce and Viv, to buy it from the township. Bruce and Viv kept saying that it didn't show as a road allowance on their survey map, only on ours. But the Township Council said it *was* a road allowance, township property, and on no account would they sell. Well then, would they close it to the public? No, they couldn't do that.

The reeve of our township came knocking on the door. That's one fabulous part of country living. When you have a problem, the reeve or the members of council come round and have a look at it. Our reeve is an Irishman and a darlin' man. We sat country-style in the kitchen and drank coffee and talked it all over. Then we went outside and looked it all over. He didn't like it. He didn't like it at all. But we both knew the council vote would go against selling. 'Not a thing I can do,' he said and went away, looking thoughtful and slightly depressed.

A week went by before he called back, very formal and official. 'I think I may have some news for you.'

'Good news?'

'I think so. You know, in my mind I kept seeing a map with a small green mark on it. That green mark means we've sold. I asked the archivist to go through the papers up here and we found it. Then we found the papers that explained it. On May

7, 1886, the township wanted a right-of-way through the land of a James Armstrong, so they arranged a swap. He gave them the land where the 7th line runs now and they gave him that road allowance. I have the original deed right here in my hand.' He nearly laughed, then recovered himself. 'We don't own it! The township doesn't own it! Hasn't owned it for ninety-nine years!'

By now I was waving the phone in the air and shouting unseemly shouts. Once recovered, I could ask, 'Who does own it?'

'Your neighbour, Bruce. Think he'd sell it to you?'

'I told you I owned it,' said Bruce. And yes, he was willing to sell—he was about to sell his entire property.

It has taken all winter, visits to the township office (we have a copy of that deed), visits to the Land Registry Office, meetings with lawyers and the Severance Council, but this spring we moved the cedar-rail fence back sixty-six feet to the foot of the hill on which Bruce had built his house. Then we planted drifts of daffodils on the worn trail.

The moral of all this is, when you buy a property, search your own title yourself, right back to the beginning of time. The lawyer thinks the man before did his homework. The surveyors think the lawyer did his homework. It's a foolish assumption to make, because, legally, they don't have to go back to the very beginning.

All this may sound as though I don't believe in the rights of the general public to shoot and walk where they will. The reason for this is that we hold title to a woods. Please note I don't say we own it. And we don't think we do in the sense that we can do whatever we please with it. Never having had the responsibility of a woods before, we took professional advice. 'Keep your feet out and your hands off' was the reply and a considerable amount of reading has underlined this advice. The world is losing species after species of living plants, trees and animals at a horrifying rate. We are destroying our own chances of survival at the same time. When I was talking about herbs so lightly, I didn't remind you that when you take your doctor's prescription to the drugstore, you walk out with foxglove or the bark of a willow tree. All those pretty pills contain plants. There are plants that may be destroyed before research can be done on them, plants that could save lives. So, though our woods is small, we intend to protect it. We think it really belongs to the fox, the porcupine, the deer and the skunk, the red-tailed hawk and the downy woodpecker, the insects and the plants. Do not disturb.

A woods does require some care. Once we acquired the land, we asked Mr. Flanagan to clean out the half-fallen dead trees and branches that would bring down healthy trees. Ten men and a pair of matched Belgians arrived. Mr. Flanagan won't take a machine into woods like ours. Too destructive. Instead, the two great horses drag a sled on wooden runners, bringing out large logs. The small branches are pulverized and tucked into hollows to turn into woods-soil. What a joy it is to watch people who know their trade! The boys swarmed up the trunks in what appeared to be tennis shoes. (No spikes. You don't want holes in your trees.) It was one of them who said, 'Please let me clean up the specimen trees standing in the open. Trees in a woods take care of themselves pretty well, but out in the open they choke themselves to death. Air and light have to reach the crotch of the branches or disease will settle in.' When he finished the maples Walter had planted and the main apple trees, you could almost see them stretch their branches and breathe. When the team had departed we walked through, and you would hardly know they had been there. Never turn a job like that over to amateurs.

Mr. Flanagan was followed by Mr. Smith to move, or rebuild, the fence. When the last fence post was to go in, deep in the woods, Mr. Smith came to Gordon and said, 'You'd better come and look.' At the end of our property line four properties meet, forming a triangle, which is the bog. It was a moot point who owned it. On the other hand, no one was arguing because no one wanted it. We call it the undisputed triangle. Gordon couldn't believe what he saw. At some time in the winter—no one heard and no one saw—the wind had reached down a hand

and, with a quick wrench and a twist, lifted a fistful of immense trees and dropped them on the triangle, creating a barricade as tall and deep as the Great Wall of China. Since neither machines nor horses can get in there, because of the surrounding quicksand, it should be some little time before it is cleared away. Though nothing would surprise me; I have seen highways, bridges, high-rises go in in worse territory. There is, just fifty feet to the south, a high-rise of sorts. It's a tall dead elm tree, left standing because the red-tailed hawk lives at the top and the trunk is riddled with the entrance doors of downy woodpeckers, squirrels, creatures uncountable. We have never touched it. Neither has the wind.

More About Apples Than You Care to Know

Today is the thirty-first of March, 38°F in the sun, bright and clear. We have just come in from pruning water-spouts out of the apple trees. Water-spouts are the branches on an apple tree that grow straight up in the air and they are the first things you should cut. Then you take out branches that rub against each other or grow at too tight an angle to the tree, trying all the while for an open airy shape. Ours are somewhat grotesque in shape because I grafted them and have been much too lax in the pruning.

It was our intention to ignore the apple trees entirely, but a man called one day; now I can remember neither his name nor what he came about. It was a pleasant day, and we sat on the retaining wall with our feet dangling in the ivy bed and talked about what we could see from there. He pointed out the irregular deep trench running along the edge of the woods and told me it was an old river bed. The water table is a lot lower now than in the days of the first settlers, and he was probably right. Then he suggested that we graft good apples onto those we had. His method was to cut the trunk straight across, about four feet from the ground, then insert the scions into the bark all around. That was too brutal and strenuous for me, and I thought it would look terrible for too long a time. When he left he said, 'I know you're going to graft those trees.' I'm easily tempted.

I bought *The Grafter's Handbook*, by R.J. Garner. It is as complicated as a course in fine carpentry, but from it I was able to choose a technique that a woman could handle. My grafting knife, with great trouble and time expended, arrived from Germany. It is an elegant little affair, with a small brass spatula for easing back the skin of the bark, many blades to choose from, its own honing stone and a special oil. The book also said that if you plant a new apple tree within twelve hundred feet of an old one, the old one will send out a virus from its roots through the earth and the new tree won't live. I didn't believe it and phoned a good nursery. Their tree man said it was perfectly true. We would have to uproot all the old trees and sterilize the earth, then wait three years to plant. 'If I were you, I'd graft.' He put me onto the Vineland Agricultural Station at Niagara and I was embarrassed to find myself in touch with Dr. Hutchinson, the chief man in charge. I explained that I was a little old lady with a few wild apple trees on a small property, but he was charmingly interested and helpful. He chose the scions that had the best chance in our Zone and phoned when they were ready to be picked up. The scions are cut before the sap runs, then held at 40°F until the trees are ready for grafting. Choose a day when the sap is running and the bark peels back like the skin of a tangerine—in late March or early April.

We went to Niagara and there we met Elf. I thought his name was Alf but no, it was Elf. He was a small man with a wicked little brown face like the shell of a walnut. He didn't want to talk to us at all. I told him I wanted to graft some trees but had never seen anything but diagrams in books. I told him what little I knew, and he said, 'Ho! Ho!' He really did say, 'Ho! Ho! Listen to her with all the fancy words, scions and such.' Suddenly he dropped all the antics and asked me to point out a tree the same size as I had. He pointed out four low branches at a good open angle to the trunk, pointing N, S, E, and W. Cut those off to a four-inch stub, he said (they were about two inches in diameter). Put three grafts on each. Leave the centre of the tree growing. That's pulling food up to keep the tree and the grafts alive. The following spring, choose the grafts that are alive and pointing in the right direction to give you a good open angle and a good tree shape. Pull the other scions out, leaving just one graft to each stub. When the grafts have grown to good-sized branches, cut out the centre of the tree. He then invited me to stay and help them graft scions onto root stock. One of my deepest regrets was that I didn't. Gordon had to be back for a meeting, but I could have stayed and thumbed my way back to Toronto. The people at Niagara are patient and helpful with the most inept amateur. If you need help, ask.

I should mention that Elf was using a broken pen-knife, which he casually sharpened on the heel of his shoe! The grafts went in so fast the tree never knew it had been cut.

Everyone asks, 'And how long before I get apples?' 'They' won't answer but I will—about three to five years. This may seem a long time, but the years before are so full of interest as you see a great knob form at the base of the graft, and a real branch bursting forth, that the waiting doesn't seem too long.

I tried one bud graft. A bud graft is a bud shaved from the scion with a thin layer of bark all round. Mine, taken from one of the scions, was about the size of a dime. I pasted it, rather awkwardly, into a dime-sized opening in the trunk because this was a one-sided tree with no branches on the south side at all. When an immense limb, growing straight up, appeared, I thought it was too big to be the graft. Now it is half the tree and produces a mysterious green apple . . . and I still don't know what it is—the tree itself or the bud graft.

Fortunately, I didn't remove the heart of our trees, because some of the varieties we were given as scions were highly susceptible to apple scab. No way am I going to spray ten times a season, so those grafts were ruthlessly cut off and destroyed before we had apple scab all through.

There's an old tale that if a tree won't bear, you just give it a good kick or hit it with a hammer. There may be something in it, for the trees that were grafted perked up and began producing their own fruit. We soon realized they couldn't be wild apples. They are our 'I don't knows'. There's an oblong yellow with a blush of pink down one side that makes the most mouth-watering apple pie you ever tasted. There's a handsome round green apple that tastes like cream of wheat and is good for nothing that we can think of. Now we are beginning to clean up, prune and feed the old trees and wait to see what we shall see. So far, no eating apples.

Apple traps and spraying with Bt. I have already described. The other preventive measure we take is picking up all the falls. Along with the Boy Scouts, we too have an Apple Day when all the family arrive with bushel baskets and wearing their old jeans. First we pick the sound fruit, and this takes longer each year, I'm happy to say. Ladders can't be used safely on our hills, so small agile grandsons climb into the trees, and as well we use the apple-picker. This is a small wire basket with five finger-like prongs curved above it. You have only to raise it on its long broomstick handle, slide the prongs over the fruit, tug, and there you are, apple in a basket. Treat your apples gently. They bruise and won't keep if they fall.

Good fruit goes into bushel baskets. Now we spread plastic drop sheets under the tree and shake. If one falls on your head, you will know how Sir Isaac Newton discovered gravity. He couldn't miss. The sheet is rolled up into a funnel and the wormy apples are shot into big green bags held open by wire supports. Bags of bad apples are hauled away in the tractor cart with the small types helping to steer or riding in back, on top of the bags. It's a great day, producing rosy cheeks, vast appetites, gallons of applesauce and dozens of apple pies. The deer stroll in a week later and clean up what we miss. Apple falls harbour all the mites and bugs you're trying to trap, so don't let them lie there and rot.

NOTES FOR THE NOVICE

Grafting

It is seldom necessary for the gardener to indulge in grafting. Roses, lilacs, many crabapples, all come ready grafted by the professionals in the nurseries. However, if you think it would be fun to try, I have suggested my best book on the subject, R.J. Garner's *The Grafter's Handbook*, and the following crash course on the veneer graft may help you make up your mind.

I used the veneer graft in order to introduce new varieties of apples into our garden. If you cut an apple open, you will find ten brown shiny seeds. Each seed contains half its genetic material from the mother tree; the other half will be from any other apple tree in the vicinity. (An apple does not know who its father was. If you plant all ten seeds, you may well produce ten different varieties of apples.) However, the fruit growing on a Spartan will all be Spartan, true to the mother tree, no matter if it was fertilized by pollen from other varieties. Often it cannot, because of a chemical barrier, fertilize itself, and so the orchardist plants several varieties to ensure cross-fertilization. If you really want to know more on this subject, try *Apples* by Peter Wynne.

The Veneer Graft

First catch your scions. You can cut them yourself while they are dormant (before the sap is running in early, early spring) or you can obtain them from a government agricultural station. They must be kept dormant, wrapped in plastic in your refrigerator at 40°F (4°C). They are thin branches about as thick through as a pencil and about 15 inches (37 cm) long. Hold them in dormancy until the sap is running and the bark ready to peel away from the trees you are grafting (mid- to late March in our area).

Prepare the tree, choosing low branches at a good open angle to the trunk and cutting them off, leaving a 4-inch (10-cm) stub. The bark of the branches you choose should be young and pliable so that you can now make a shallow 1-inch (2.5-cm) slit straight out to the edge (three or four of these evenly spaced). With your spatula peel back two flaps of the bark, one on each side of the slit, to give you a triangular opening.

Cut the scions into 5-inch (12-cm) lengths as you go so they won't dry out. With the buds pointing *up*, shave one side of the bottom in a ¾-inch (2-cm) slanting out. Now gently, gently, shave an infinitesimal strip from both sides of the slant so that you can see a fine green stripe. (In grafting, you are wedding

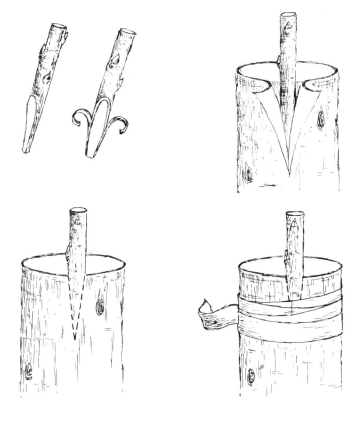

cambium layer to cambium layer, but as it is invisible and just under the green, I use the green stripe to guide me. Match the green of scion and tree and you have matched the cambium layers.)

Slide the cut end of the scion down under the flaps, raw side against tree. Then, using a thumb nail, groove each flap tight into the side of the scion. With your grafting knife, cut along this groove, tight to the scion so that it makes a close fit, removing extra bark as you cut.

When all three (or four) scions are firmly in place, wrap them in tightly with grafting tape and then smarm the whole thing over with grafting wax. Have the wax sitting in a pail of hot water so that you can knead it into shape. Cover your hands and wrists first with olive oil or you'll be in a terrible sticky mess. I leave the waxing until all grafts are taped in position.

The following spring, if you have done your work well, you will see that most of your grafts have taken. Don't be in too much of a hurry about this, but once you are certain the best ones are alive and growing, remove all the others, leaving on each stub one healthy little scion turning itself into a new branch. Sometimes they grow happily for a year or two, filling you with hope, then fall off. Not your fault: tree and scion were incompatible.

Equipment: sharp small knife, spatula, grafting tape and grafting wax.

Source: mail-order houses and large nurseries.

Cutting It Down to Size

One of the first books the young gardener should buy is a book on pruning. Usually it is the last, and by then it may well be too late. It is the early, constant and skilled trimming and thinning that keeps trees, shrubs and evergreens in shape. Left to their own devices, they may grow to the point where they are past saving and must be replaced or, as in the case of some shrubs, whacked off at ground level, and you must wait for them to grow again. It is usually the foundation planting—the first and most expensive investment in the garden—which suffers this sad fate.

When both garden and gardener are brand new, a veritable forest of greenery is rushed in (Instant Garden Syndrome), and very nice it looks, too. The professional—the amateur as well for that matter—wants a finished look for the first planting. The difficulty is that the plants haven't finished. They have barely started, and the three-foot shrub in the four-foot space grows to six feet. Overplanting, too much too soon, chokes up many a garden and the bewildered owner may wonder why he isn't happy with it. Pruning, he is told, is the answer; and so it is, but it is only part of the answer. In some instances, digging up and throwing away, thinning out the overgrowns and the past-its, or transplanting the six-foot shrub to a ten-foot space can work miracles. What will not work miracles is a violent attack with the electric hedge-trimmer. A woman who would not dream of allowing her husband to give her a haircut will send him forth with a hedge-trimmer to wreak havoc in the garden. It is assumed that because he knows how the tool works he will know what to do with it. He won't. In actual fact, he should confine its use to hedges, hedges only, and not every hedge at that.

May I suggest a book? My most recent acquisition is *Pruning*

Simplified, by Lewis Hill. Mr. Hill does simplify the subject to the best of his ability, which is considerable, if not awesome. The sheer weight of information may confuse, unless you follow his suggestion of reading only the first four chapters, after that restricting yourself to looking up the tree, shrub or evergreen that concerns you. Then, if you pay attention, you will soon learn that as the twig is clipped, the tree will grow. Cut to an outside leaf and the new growth will move out in the direction the leaf points. Cut to an inside leaf, and the new growth will move in to the centre.

Not everything is pruned in the same way, or at the same time of year, or to the same purpose. Shearing the outside growth to a smooth curve on a Brown's yew will encourage thick, bushy growth. If you want open, airy growth, remove dead, broken, or diseased stems at the ground line and then cut out a quarter of the old growth. This would renew and add to the natural grace of a forsythia.

However, if the subject of your concern is an Antony Waterer spiraea, *all* the old growth should be cut back to three inches in late winter or early spring, freeing up the new green growth as it appears. Bloom will appear on this new growth this season.

On the other hand, if the spiraea is *thunbergii*, don't prune it until it has produced its tiny, delicate white blooms along the thin arching branches and these have dropped. Then you can thin out the older branches at the ground line, leaving the young and springy and making room for new. This shrub blooms on last year's growth, which means that it will bloom next year on the branches that develop this year. Confusing, isn't it? Actually, it's only confusing when you read about it. Once you have performed the exercise, all will be clear as clear, which is true of all pruning. Most of us are too rash or too fearful. Whichever you are, I suggest practice on wild growth at the summer cottage or on something frightful in your own garden.

None of that is meant as a guide to pruning: it is simply to persuade you that you do need help. You must know *why* you are making the cut, *how* to make the cut, the tool to use and, most of all, *what* it is that you are cutting.

For guidance, you may prefer the brief pamphlet, with step-by-step instructions and diagrams. Your Department of Agriculture can provide these on apple trees, raspberries, deciduous trees, evergreens and even roses. Simple diagrams can be found in a good nursery catalogue. They all stress the basic principles:

1. Remove dead wood at any time.
2. Remove broken and diseased branches at any time.
3. For full pruning, identify the tree or shrub and prune when dormant (e.g., apple trees in March before the sap is running; maple trees six weeks before frost, late enough not to stimulate new, soft growth, which would winter-kill.)
4. Select those branches that delineate the shape you are after and remove the rest, remembering that you can throw a tree into shock with too drastic pruning. The operation can be carried out over a two-to-three-year period.
5. Young trees need gentle yearly attention.

Tools required include secateurs (hand clippers), loppers, shears, pruning saws (curved and straight); all kept clean and sharp.

When studying all these books and pamphlets, you will begin to detect a certain enthusiasm, a religious zeal; there can be no doubt that their authors *like* to prune. This is their calling in life. Should you not fall into this category, there are certain ploys you can use; you can side-step, parry and evade, though you can never escape entirely. When you reflect that most of this vigorous activity has to be timed for early, early spring (ankle-deep in snow) or late fall (when the weather is chill and dismal) and you are weighed down with other garden chores as well, any ruse that will lighten the load should be welcome.

Buy the right plant. A beauty bush spreads to fifteen feet, a mugho pine aspires to be a five-foot tree, the savin juniper arches out to six feet in width. Each plant bears a label stating its ultimate height and width. You will be told that, with constant shearing and pruning, it can be held back. I don't know how fond you are of constant pruning and shearing. You will also be told that it will take five to ten years for the plant to reach this size. You are still planning to be around then, one supposes, so why store up trouble? Allow not only for the ultimate height and width but for extra space as well, to set the plant off.

If space does not allow, choose the slow-grower, the easily controlled, such as yew, the amenable box, the neat, sturdy pine and the well-behaved sugar maple. Finding the right plant can be like finding the right man, but the plant does wear a label, and you can look it up. Try not to be led astray by appearance and charm. Character is all. The books will tell you all about the bad habits of poplar, willow and Manitoba maple. Read and be warned. The fast-growers, the invasive, the overbearing and the sloppy can all be barred from your garden. The growers have now developed evergreens that are bred to behave. These are labelled *nana* or *compacta*, meaning dwarfed. Oddly enough, the word 'dwarf' is not always to be trusted, but if the price sends you staggering back into the pots and jars, you can be sure you have found the genuine article. These evergreens can be obtained usually only from the nurseries specializing in dwarfed plants: charming small pines, junipers and yews, which will serve you for years in small spaces.

Lastly, underplant. You can always make additions. When you find yourself paying $150 for the removal of something that cost you $38.53, it is the time of the gnashing of teeth. Recently, with the aid of two men and a large boy, we removed two little cotoneasters from the shrub border. They had taken over all the dwarf deutzia in a ten-by-eight-foot space. After much wrenching and digging, the two main roots were found. In the end, a strong rope was fastened to a root and then tied to the back axle of a truck. As the truck drove slowly off in low gear, half the root, most of the stone curbing, and long strips of the lawn came away. Throughout this same border, cheaper material had been interplanted to be removed later. When we came to the removal, we found that these poorer plants had the place of honour. Everything had to be lifted and transplanted. Don't do as I did. Do as I say. Underplant!

Or don't plant it at all. This advice came from Amy. We stood at the bottom of the stairs leading to the pool and agreed that all those great lumps of evergreens edging the stairs did not belong. They had to go.

'What can I plant in their place?' We studied the problem at length and in silence and then Amy came up with the faultless answer.

'Nothing,' she said.

Space, the contour of a hill, the unbroken sweep of green, the changing sky bring serenity to a garden and provide the setting for the perfect tree or the quiet pond. And think of this: if you don't plant it, you won't have to prune it.

NOTES FOR THE NOVICE

Pruning

THE BASIC CUT

The basic cut should be clean, sharp and slanted. The idea is to leave no crevice, shreds of bark, or shelf to hold moisture where disease and insect life can take hold. Slant out from the top towards the ground to shed rain.

When dealing with a large branch, first cut the weight away at about 12 inches (30 cm) from the trunk. You will see a ring of wrinkled bark where the branch joins the trunk. Slice upward in front of the ring about one-third of the way through. Now reverse the saw and (still in front of the ring) cut down at a slant to join the upward slice. The ring, left in place, will callous and heal much more quickly than if you had cut flush with the trunk. The first upward cut prevents the tearing of bark.

To paint or not to paint is up to the individual. I don't because the paint dries, lifts and leaves a haven for disease. But if I find a tree running sap from wind or rodent damage, I paint with *orange* shellac (other shellacs may burn).

TREES

Leave the major pruning of tall, full-grown trees to a professional and be sure he is just that.

SHRUBS

Some shrubs should be pruned in late winter to early spring, before they show green: i.e., buddleia, hydrangea or false spiraea. However, *Buddleia alternifolis*, along with deutzia, lilac and *Spiraea thunbergii*, should be pruned after they have bloomed. Identification is important.

The pruning of most shrubs really consists of thinning. Take out dead branches, broken branches and diseased wood close to the ground. If the plant still looks choked up, remove some of the older branches, especially those that are crossed in to the centre. But it is wiser to remove only a quarter to a third of the older growth in most cases, or you may destroy the shrub. Only then should you stand back and picture the final shape you are after and cut back a few branches at the tips.

All that sounds like such a gentle exercise. In reality, you should be clad in heavy slacks, long-sleeved shirt, leather gloves and goggles (a full-grown shrub is not above giving you a poke in the eye). Armed with clippers, long and short, pruning saw, and long-handled loppers, you will look as though you are about to invade enemy territory through a barbed-wire fence, and the experience is not unlike. It involves dropping to your knees and scouting the undergrowth, which may well be a thick tangle of long grass and weeds. This has to be cleared away before you can even see the base of the branches. Reaching the base of the branches involves lying flat on your stomach and wriggling in to see which branch to tackle with the heavy loppers. Loppers slip and the handles can bounce off your nose; for this reason, I always keep the handles horizontal to the ground. All this really does sound discouraging, which is why it is rarely mentioned.

THE ROSE

Let us begin with pruning a rose. I am assuming that you have never ever pruned anything.

It should have been earthed up for the winter and now the earth has been gently teased away so as not to snap off the fat little pink buds. Not all of the bush was covered by earth, as the owner wisely did not prune it back in the fall. All of each cane not protected by earth is obviously dead; the lower half of each cane is green, bearing the aforesaid pink buds. These buds will turn into side branches and bear roses. You want the branch to grow out from the centre, so you choose a top bud that grows *out* and make your cut above that. The cut should slant slightly down towards the centre and be about ¼ inch (6 mm) above the bud. (See drawing.) Using clean, sharp snippers (secateurs), repeat this operation with each cane. Any canes that are completely dead should be cut close to earth level.

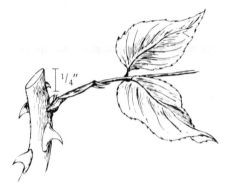

In early spring, the North American practice is to cut the canes back to 4 or 5 inches (10–12 cm) from the ground. This should encourage strong canes to spring up from just above the graft. However, I know of two English gardeners, living in Ontario, who start their roses out at a 10- to 12-inch (25–30 cm) height with great success: larger bushes and more roses. As well, they mulch with well-rotted manure. With such conflicting advice, it might pay the beginning gardener to try both methods: high pruning and natural manure on one bed, the low cut and treated manure on the other. See what works for you.

Later in the season, one is often advised to prune back to the fifth leaf from the bottom (if it faces *out*), but I often prune higher. A new, spindly plant has only the dead bloom clipped at the base of the flower to give it the opportunity of fattening out with lots of leaves. Leaves manufacture the food that strengthens the roots; without strong roots you won't have vigorous bloom. On the whole it pays to purchase a strong, healthy cultivar at the beginning.

Encourage each plant to develop three or four strong canes. You can clear out small leaves, low down and crowding the centre, to allow air circulation.

To return to that slanting cut, above an *out*-growing leaf and towards the centre: perfect it and continue to use it on your shrubs and all your plants.

Dividing

Years are spent coaxing, feeding and persuading everything to grow, and then you may begin to wonder if you have overdone it. There is no elbow room! Trimming back has done all that it can do. The time has come to *divide*. This means lifting the plant and breaking or cutting it into smaller sections. Replant what you wish to keep in fresh earth and throw away or give away the leftovers.

CHRYSANTHEMUMS

In late spring, lift, wash and divide into three or four outside sections and discard the older centre, which won't bloom well. The outside sections can be replanted or potted up for setting out again in the fall, unless you have a bed that is strictly for chrysanthemums. Or bring them out and on stage just before the curtain falls in September–October.

DAY LILIES

In four to five years, day-lily clumps can grow to be enormous. I would rather lift and divide an old shrub. Have a man with a strong back handy. The roots are not deep, but they are wide, dense and heavy. You may be able to split them with a spade, but on my last try I used a pruning saw.

IRIS

August is the time to divide and replant the tall bearded variety. (The Siberian are sufficiently hardy to be replanted in late September, in shade.) The rhizome of the bearded iris, like a sweet potato, will often break apart easily. Wash first so that you can see clearly any evidence of soft or diseased parts, which may be cut away before the sound parts are replanted. Plant shallowly, a foot (30 cm) apart and in straight rows. (They will arrange their own clumps.)

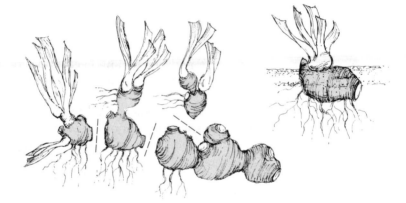

PEONIES

Don't divide unless you are desperate for more of that particular variety and can't purchase it. I am too old to wait about for a three- to five-eye plant to bloom, so I buy ten- to twelve-eye. The 'eye' is a pointed ruby bud at the top of the root and should be no more than 2 inches (5 cm) below the earth surface.

PHLOX

These need dividing every three to four years. In late fall, when through blooming, cut the plant back to 8 inches (20 cm). Lift and split with a spade. Some growers divide to four or five stems. Again, I prefer larger divisions.

Delphinium, columbine and other perennials in our climate keep to size or die out. Keep a steady supply of new plants coming on to replace them. If you are putting the divisions or new plants in old places, remove the old earth and replace with new from your vegetable garden or compost pile. Earth benefits from being moved about, but so do plants, and this dividing exercise may be a fine chance to redesign your borders.

Dead-Heading

When a flower is flossing about in full bloom, look at it closely. All those frilly ruffles and perfume are simply intended for bee bait. The bee arrives and enters the flower, picking up pollen on its fuzzy coat from the stamens (little stems within the flower, which surround a strong central stem, the pistil). The pollen brushes off onto the pistil, then travels down to the calyx below the flower and there impregnates the seed within. The seed begins to grow and the plant now focusses all its interest on the seed, forgets about frills and perfume, and turns up at the breakfast table looking frowsty. To prevent, or at least post-pone, this sorry state of affairs, the gardener steps in and dead-heads the plant. That is, he removes *both* the dead flower and its seed. (I'm sure your mother gave you the gist of all this).

PETUNIAS: With scissors or thumb and finger, nip the dead flower off below the little green cup that supports it.

MARIGOLDS: The seeds are in the petals, so just remove the head and stem.

PHLOX: Cut off the flower head (the seeds are in the little flow-erettes) and the side shoots will bloom.

DAY LILIES, DELPHINIUMS, TULIPS: Cut the stem right to the ground when all bloom is over. Individual blooms (as in day lilies) can be cut or snapped off. Don't remove the leaves.
Now you have the idea. Remove the seed.
BUT DON'T REMOVE THE BUD!

LILAC: When blooming has finished, you cut the bloom head off through the green stem. Just below it you will see a brown twin-set of buds. This is next year's bloom. Take every care to leave these in place.

HEUCHERA (CORAL BELLS): In the spring this plant will be a mound of dry leaves and you will be tempted to trim it back. Don't. Just ruffle it with the palm of your hand and let the wind blow the chaff away. The buds of those long-stemmed bells are in there somewhere, so no trimming.

For other plants, use your eyes and let the plant tell you which is seed and which is bud. Remove seeds and preserve buds. This will keep your whole garden looking like bee bait.

Basic Recipe for a Wedding in a Garden

Can there be a good basic recipe for a wedding? The etiquette books and the wedding bureaus have been working at it for years, yet I have known several marriages that set beautifully after being whipped up in three seconds at the city hall. Weddings are as unique and original as the people who engage in them, so the following is offered only on the understanding that it is to be modified, expanded or seasoned to taste.

INGREDIENTS

Mix in equal parts:
>   The people you love: This may have to be reduced to the people you love a *lot*.
>   Superlative food: Catered and pre-tested or, if your strength is as the strength of ten, home-prepared.
>   The very best wines.
>   The very, very best champagne.
>   Flowers: Do not stint here
>   Music: Live or taped

Pour carefully into a garden on a summer day and later top with a dark sky and stars.

That appears to be simple and attractive but, as Michael Field advised with many of his recipes, 'Do not attempt this alone. Have twelve Brownies in the kitchen to peel the onions and chop the nuts.' You will require:

1. A Girl Friday: In charge of caterers, bartenders, florists, car-

penters, electricians, hairdresser, the bride, you, the whole family, and guests.

2. A Music Producer: Pre-test live groups. Is their material danceable, digestible or censorable? Flutes or recorders are enchanting at a small affair but may be too thin in the open air. Tapes will give you everything from Bach to rock and can be cut to fit.

3. A Producer: In charge of pre-service and rehearsal of service. If you have a strong-minded cousin, uncle or son with a stopwatch, who will hold everyone firmly in line until it's precisely as bride and groom want it, engage him.

EQUIPMENT:

One marquee in case of rain (unless the house will hold the teeming throng). If you go for a marquee, stipulate clearly that you will not accept one that has been dragged through a wet field.

One dance floor: If you are marrying off Aunt Hattie (80) to Joe's dad (85), you can skip this. Otherwise, stipulate clearly that it is to be danced on; therefore, reinforced and supported to lie flat on the grass.

Round tables: For no less than eight. And place cards. The whole world will come apart over the place cards. (If you put a napkin in the wine glass and the card in the napkin, it will not blow away.) Their purpose—and you, the bride and the groom will work long hours on this—is to see that all guests are sitting with someone they know and like or with whom they have something in common. The VIPs at any party are the guests.

Chairs, glasses, china, cutlery, cloths, stoves: Your Girl Friday will coordinate all these, but you and the bride should see a sample of each.

Flowers: Pre-test. If the florist is good at funerals—run! Look, seek, ask until you find one with imagination and flair to set the stage with gaiety and charm.

The Garden: The grass should be manicured to the nth about three days before so that it softens up around the edges and clippings blow away. Feed, weed and water the flower beds a week before—but a little magic may work its way in here. Why did the early peonies, the mid-season and the late single Carrara all come into full bloom on that same day in late June? The lilacs were finished and trimmed, but why were other early shrubs still flossing about in their finery? And the roses with no roots? You would have thought they had roots to China. Your flowers won't fail you.

We had one other mystery: the day before The Day, I found hundreds, thousands of bees boiling like toffee all over the ajuga in the shrub border, scarcely two feet from the open wall of the marquee. I had promised that, just this once, I would spray for flies, mosquitoes and anything else that stings or bites. But the bees? How could I spray the bees? Move the marquee? It was on the only flat space we had.

Ah! A wedding! And I hadn't told them. So I told them. They went on bumbling around, paying no attention. So I became more explicit. They were asked not to go roistering around on the wedding cake or the guests—most particularly not the guests.

They didn't come to the wedding at all. Not one bee. Didn't even send their regrets. Whether they took offence—I had, after all, implied that they would not know how to comport themselves on a formal occasion—or whether they don't care for music. . . . now that I think of it, there were no flies or mosquitoes either. Must have been the wind.

A Gathering of Gardens

Nancy C.'s garden is a group of still lifes. She creates pictures in shapes and colours. The best example is a huge white shell shape, planted to Pink Cascade petunias, on the back terrace. Just beyond it is a controlled oval bed of pink phlox to pick up the colour. A few hanging baskets above it in a deeper rose and she has her composition. An hour of watering and attending to dead heads can keep it in a state of perfection.

In the deep shade, along the walk to the front door, she plants impatiens, that obliging plant, which shapes itself to the space it is meant to fill. Deep in this planting is a nice old stump with vines growing over it.

Keep it simple, says Nancy.

Gene's garden is a fabulous tumble of all the flowers in the world, in fine health, clambering up a slope, sliding down another, having such a wonderful time, but held in control by a neat hedge here or an easy, relaxed edging.

Vines climb over an old-fashioned well-head, bucket and all. St. Francis stands in the niche of a tall slim stump, surrounded by vines and always by birds. They alight on his head and, occasionally, on Gene's as well.

Keep it happy, says Gene.

Amy is a plantswoman. Her vast garden holds rare plants side by side with others that are easily recognizable, but each is precisely where it wants to be, in its own kind of soil, with its own kind of climate, and its owner can call it by its correct Latin name in the flick of an eyelash. As they come and go, they combine to create a pattern as intricate and pleasing as a fine Oriental carpet.

Know your plants, says Amy.

The doctor's garden I saw long ago. A wide, shallow suburban backyard had been planted around three sides with beautiful tall specimens of evergreen trees, dropping their wide skirts down to brush the grass. They stepped forward or swung back to create deep bays, in front of them only a perfectly manicured turf. Across the back of the house a stone terrace had been built full width, divided by three wide stone steps. On either side of the steps were two deep and long beds, entirely filled with well-tended roses. That was it. The doctor was a specialist and his specialty was roses. Someone else manicured the lawn.

Keep it serene, said the doctor.

Ro's is a painter's garden. She inherited, from Barbara, a fine collection of perennials in good health, but confessed nervously that she knew nothing about gardening. Would I help? It was weeks before I got to her, and then I stood open-mouthed. She had spent the afternoons sitting on the long porch, painting the border and pond before her. As she painted she would think, the yellow should be over in that corner, the tall plant moved to the left; then she would dash down and move them, returning to her painting and saying, that's better. She moved shrubs to clear the view to the pond, tossed in waterlilies, and accomplished all this at the wrong time of year, the wrong way: moving, pruning and planting with blithe insouciance. The whole planting was thriving and preening itself. It knew it was picture perfect.

Look for balance, line and colour. *Look* at your garden, says Ro.

As you visit your friends' gardens you may feel a twinge of envy. Weed it out. Envy and one-upmanship don't belong in a garden. Someone will always have a more beautiful garden, a better design, a taller delphinium. It doesn't matter. Whether you know it or not, your own garden will be like you and in all probability you yourself won't know what it's saying.

A man, a total stranger, gave me the clue to mine. He walked out the back and looked at the view. 'I know another garden with this kind of setting,' he said, 'It's the most beautiful garden I ever saw. Yours is different.' He looked thoughtful. I was wondering if I was going to get a C −, but then a light bulb popped on and he said, 'I've got it. You use it. You hold parties down there and people can eat at tables over there or the family can gather here. He smiled at me, 'You use it, don't you? You use it.' I think I got a C+.

And I suppose that's what it is—a people garden. You can lie on the grass and let it absorb whatever it is that ails you; or you can, if you like, slide downhill on a tin tray in the snow, yelling your head off. You can float in the pool, lie in the hammock, go off by yourself in the woods, or sit around the tables by candlelight and talk with your friends. A people garden. I gave myself a B.

The Trug

I had long admired the trug that sits on the floor of Sonia's and Hugh's restaurant. It was not for sale, and I couldn't blame her. She had seen my covetous eyes cast upon it and explained what it was for. Not for weeds. It was for the gentle art of gathering long-stemmed flowers, and one should really be suitably attired in a wide-brimmed hat and floating gown.

Hugh called one afternoon to say they had reserved a table for us; if we came that night we could meet his sister from England. When we walked in the door we could see which was our table. The usual 'Bespoke' sign wasn't there. What was there was the most elegant of trugs, overflowing with garden produce. I was promptly posed on a bench, trug in lap, and had my picture taken. We met his sister and heard the tale of 'The Trug Hunt', as she called it. To begin with, she didn't know what a trug was and none of her friends knew either. Once that information was forthcoming, probably from Sonia, the problem was to find one. Only two places in England made them at that time. Hugh's sister set out to visit both places, deciding finally that the finest were those from the estate of the Duke of Westminster: no splinters, hand-made and the over-lapping laths held to the frame with copper studs. After all that, she refused to entrust it to the baggage people and had flown across the Atlantic with my trug sitting in her lap.

Grateful and impressed as I was, I couldn't bear to use it. It sat for a long time beside a pine cabinet where it could be admired. But last summer, setting out to cut flowers, I picked it up and stepped out into the garden. The first flower was picked and laid with its head resting on the rim. Glancing back at the border, I could immediately see precisely the flower that should lie beside it. The whole arrangement came to life in the trug, everything decided before the flowers went into the vase. Extraordinary.

Perhaps it is not too extraordinary. The trug was designed for just this purpose by Thomas Smith about a hundred and fifty years ago, and the first one was made at Horns House in the village of Herstmonceaux, Sussex. This workshop is still in existence. One of its first orders came from Queen Victoria, and now it supplies those sold at the estate of the Duke of Westminster.

I have since seen trugs for sale in St. Andrews, New Brunswick, and in Oakville, Ontario—a little rough and splintery compared to mine, but the right shape. Once a few gardeners try them the word will get around and you will all want one.

Mine had been meant as a symbol, a sign that the day would come—and then it came sooner than I thought. Gordon walked in from the garden and announced that he would have to buy a new shovel. 'The old one broke. Funny thing. I put it in the cart, drove up the hill, and when I took it out, only half of it was there. I can't find the other half.' It was the long-handled shovel from the first garden.

I went out to make sure. I hate goodbyes. When I saw it lying there in the gravel beside the garbage bins and thought of all we had been through together, the good times and the rough times, I felt the twinge of parting. The shovel just looked tired.

Was it the end of an era? When I turned away I remembered the trug. Was it time now to slide an arm through that graceful hoop, balance the fingers lightly on the far rim and stroll about, gathering the black-eyed Susans and the Queen Anne's lace? It is an idyllic vision, but there are days now when it comes true, when the garden, the trug and I decide, all evidence to the contrary, that this is all there is to do. I just might buy a wide-brimmed, ribbon-bedecked straw hat to wear for these occasions and, at long last, garden like a lady.

Summer Afternoon

On a warm day in late summer, September only a breath away, I sit down by the pool and look back up at the house. The roses are raising their lovely heads in their last burst of bloom before the cold winds come.

But I have work to do. I have avoided this as long as I can. Too long. I must learn the names of all the plants, their correct names, and that means Latin.

I am not looking forward to this. I am at an age when it is all I can do to remember what day it is, and now I intend to memorize the genera, species and variety of every plant I grow? The only good thing to be said for it is that it can be done sitting down.

To assist me in this doubtful enterprise I have two texts, both by Liberty H. Bailey: *How Plants Get Their Names* and *Manual of Cultivated Plants*, which is really a reference book, an encyclopedia of almost everything that grows. They both tend to be formidable and, if you can find an easier way I recommend it, whatever it is. Start at least forty years ahead of me, while your memory is sharp and you have fewer plants.

But I enjoy Dr. Bailey. He retired the year I was born and died in the late sixties, having published nearly seventy books in his ninety-year span. His voice is gentle, amused, and persuasive. If I may quote him: ''To know the names of the forms of life is one of the keenest satisfactions . . . '' He goes on to explain that the correct name is far from enough. It must be attached to the correct plant. (We can all cite frightful examples of the correct label on the wrong plant. The nursery blames the grower and the grower blames the bees . . . or the help he gets these days.) So ordering by the Latin name won't always ensure that you get what you ordered. That's not the point. The point, as he says, is the truth. And so the gardener-student must study the plant along with its name.

With the aid of good reading glasses and a magnifying glass, I am able, at last, to name the little green plant that came to me accidentally from Mary's garden. Gene said it was woodruff and I said it looked like baby's breath. Gene is right. It is in the same family as woodruff, *Rubiaceae* (the madder family). But it is *Galium*, not *Rubia*. Mine is *Galium mollugo* (white bedstraw or false baby's-breath). So I am right, too. It was used in the making of pallets or beds or, according to Dioscorides, for the curdling of milk. It can be found growing as a weed in fields in the eastern United States and Canada. If you would like to look for it, I can describe it to you. It grows as a little shrub, one to two feet high. The thin green stem is square and the leaves grow in groups of eight in whorls around the stem, approximately two inches apart. The leaf is one-half to one inch long, with a single line or nerve down the centre. Should it be in bloom, the flowers will look like the fine white baby's-breath. One small root will grow into a neat round plant for you, from which you can take divisions and build up a hedge or give some away to friends. It behaves itself nicely in the garden and is exquisite with sweet peas.

Mr. Bailey has also explained my *Helleborus niger*, the Christmas rose. In a cold climate it will arrange to bloom in the spring. The first plant, which Mardi brought to me frozen solid, still bravely blooms under two feet of snow, but that is because it is closer to the house and is led astray by the warmth of the wall.

The book is heavy and the sun is warm. Before me, the hill rises away from the pool and this is where the field wildflowers grow. There is a clump of honeysuckle near the top, and beneath these Miranda lies buried. She was thirteen years in this garden and her small ghost haunts it still, hiding under the hedge, lying on her rock in the sun. There are other ghosts, other memories; all the people who have come with advice, a shrub, a blue delphinium, my favourite lily, filling the garden with their merriment and nonsense this summer, summers past and summers to come.

I am startled out of my musings. Simon has been crouched

in the long grass of the hill, nose to ground, nearly invisible.

'What have you found, Simon?'

'A BUG!!' It is the discovery of the century. He explodes out of the grass, small fists waving.

David goes over to see and they bring me, balanced on David's finger, a primeval monster, a bulging-eyed prehistoric dragon a quarter of an inch long.

'What is it?' David asks.

'A bug.'

My grandson retrieves it and returns to the hill, pleased to have his identification substantiated, but David gives me that long look with one eyebrow raised, reminiscent of his grandfather, and I feel guilty. Well now, dammit, am I supposed to know the proper name of every bug, bird, plant and flower on the place? Any garden, no matter how large or small, can lead you down so many distracting paths, into entomology, ornithology, or the specialized study of one genera and species in the plant world. You can become a rosarian or a crocusist. There has to be a limit.

I have decided not to pursue the study of bugs. An aphid, a rose chafer, a ladybug (or ladybird) I know. Apart from that I'm with Simon. A bug's a bug. Sometimes, a BUG!

But now Karina is alerting us all, pointing an accusing finger at the sky. 'Look! Oh, Look! There he goes! The strawberry bird!' It is the robin who pecks holes in the strawberries, but no one corrects her. We like her name better anyway. So, some of the birds have their right names and some haven't.

And the trees? The shrubs? The flowers? Some have their common names and some answer to Latin, as you have already guessed. I shall do my best, I think, with great resolution, and glance sideways at Dr. Bailey's book; then realize that of all the people who ever lived he would be the most forgiving. Still, I *shall* do my best, and for the rest, people must ask the questions to which I have the answer.

But here is Edward, blissfully inebriated on warm milk and hot sun. He is full of purpose and has some goal in mind. Ah yes, my lap. My grandmother had a lap like a featherbed, but mine requires a bounce or two to soften it up before he can settle down.

Simon has returned the bug with reverent care to its blade of grass and carried my glance once more up to the hill. The field daisy, the hawkweed, viper's bugloss, mullein and St. Johns-wort, flecks of colour in the spiky green, mist the hill to its top and shimmer away out of sight into the wild apple trees on the right, an exercise in pointillism, a Seurat, a Monet. On the left we have rebuilt the steps down to the pool, wider as Walter wanted them, and soon the tide of wildflowers will wash up against them as Amy suggested.

This meadow does not depend on me for its existence, nor do other parts of the garden. Trees rise from the unmown grass and step out of the woods; elm, sugar maple, and trembling aspen. Where I meant to plant pussy willows in a group of white pine, I find two already there. The elm is the best surprise. This was an area where Dutch elm disease had devastated the land-scape, and now young elms, some fifteen feet high, apparently healthy and strong, are appearing. The garden arranges itself, rounding out the straight edges, filling in a blank space, never static, never still, ever changing. It takes a while to realize what has happened and then I must tell someone.

I tell Edward. ''The land has healed itself.''

He makes a comfortable noise. He has yet to unravel the magic and mystery of words. English or Latin, it is all one to Edward. But he is a wise child and knows how we should occupy ourselves on a summer afternoon . . . lean back and contemplate the passing of a cloud, hear the bird call, and watch the leaves turn.

Sources and Suppliers

Many of the growers listed here will ship from coast to coast. Of course you can always drive about the countryside, call in, and choose your very own. Whatever you do, send for catalogues. They are highly educational and make for inspirational reading in the winter. And don't let appearances fool you: some of the best suppliers send out the dreariest catalogues. Good hunting.

ALBERTA

Alberta Nurseries and Seeds Ltd.
Box 20
Bowden, Alta.
T0M 0K0

Beaverlodge Nursery
Box 127
Beaverlodge, Alta.
T2N 0E8

Cheyenne Tree Farms
Box 8704, Station L
Edmonton, Alta.
T6C 4J5

Mountain View Nursery
1007 2nd Ave.
Calgary, Alta.
T2N 0E8

Windy Ridge Nursery
Box 301
Hythe, Alta.
T0H 2C0

BRITISH COLUMBIA

Nurseries—General

Cannor Nurseries Ltd.
48291 Chilliwack Central Rd.
R. R. 1
Chilliwack, B.C.
V2P 6H3

Les Clay & Son Ltd.
Box 3040
Langley, B.C.
V3A 4R3

Homestead Nurseries Ltd.
Wright Rd.
Clayburn, B.C.
V0X 1E0

Art Knapp's Plantland
6250 Lougheed Hwy.
Burnaby, B.C.
V5B 2Z9

Massot Nurseries
16060 Westminster Hwy.
Richmond, B.C.
V6V 1A8

Seeds

Buckerfield's Seeds
P. O. Box 1030
Abbotsford, B.C.
V2S 5B5

Butchart Gardens
Box 4010, Station A
Victoria, B.C.
V8X 3X4

Rocky Mountain Seed Service
Box 215
Golden, B.C.
V0A 1H0

Sanctuary Seeds
2388 West 4th Ave.
Vancouver, B.C.
V6K 1P1

Miniatures

Miniature Plant World
45638 Elder Ave.
Sardis, B.C.
V2R 1A5

MANITOBA

Aubin Nurseries
P. O. Box 268
Carmen, Man.
R0G 0J0

Boughen Nurseries
Box 12
Valley River, Man.
R0L 2B0

Canadian Garden Products
(Thompson & Morgan Seeds)
160117 King Edward St.
Winnipeg, Man.
R3H 0Y3

Koop Nursery
Kleefield, Man.
R0A 0V0

McFayden
P. O. Box 1800
30 9th St.
Brandon, Man.
R7A 6N4

NEW BRUNSWICK

Halifax Seed Co. Ltd.
Box 2021
664 Rothesay Ave.
Saint John, N.B.
E2L 3T5

The Herb Farm
R. R. 4
Norton, N.B.
E0G 2N0

NEWFOUNDLAND

Gaze Seed Co. Ltd.
P.O. Box 640
St. John's, Nfld.
A1C 5K8

NOVA SCOTIA

Halifax Seed Co. Ltd.
Box 8026
5860 Kane St.
Halifax, N.S.
B3K 5L8

Maritime Nurseries Ltd.
Box 10
Falmouth, N.S.
B0P 1L0

Milligan Bros. Ltd.
Waverley
Halifax County, N.S
B0N 2S0

Rawlinson Garden Seed
269 College Rd.
Truro, N.S.
B2N 2P6

ONTARIO

Nurseries—General

John Connon Nurseries
Highway 5
Waterdown, Ont.
L0R 2H0

Hortico Inc.
R. R. 1
723 Robson Rd.
Waterdown, Ont.
L0R 2H0

Humber Nurseries Ltd.
R. R. 8
Brampton, Ont.
L6T 3Y7

Sheridan Nurseries
700 Evans Ave.
Etobicoke, Ont.
M9C 1A1

Perennials

McMillen's Iris Garden
R. R. 1
Norwich, Ont.
N0J 1P0

The Country Squire's Garden
Steeles Ave.
R. R. 10
Brampton, Ont.
L6V 3N2

Stirling Perennials
R. R. 1
Morpeth, Ont.
N0P 1X0

Woodland Nurseries
(rhododendrons and azaleas)
2151 Camilla Rd.
Mississauga, Ont.
L5A 2K1

Seeds

W. R. Aimers Ltd.
(wildflower seeds)
Cotswolds, The Green Lane
R. R. 1
King City, Ont.
L0G 1K0

William Dam Seeds
(organic)
Box 8400
Dundas, Ont.
L9H 6M1

Stokes Seeds Ltd.
39 James St., Box 10
St. Catharines, Ont.
L2R 6R6

Bulbs

C. A. Cruikshank Inc.
1015 Mount Pleasant Rd.
Toronto, Ont.
M4P 2M1

Gardenimport Inc.
P. O. Box 760
Thornhill, Ont.
L3T 4A5

Dwarf Evergreens

Mori Gardens
R. R. 2
Niagara-on-the-Lake, Ont.
L0S 1J0

Oslach Nurseries Inc.
Green's Corners
R. R. 1
Simcoe, Ont.
N3Y 4J9

Vineland Nurseries
P. O. Box 98
Vineland Station, Ont.
L0R 2E0

Herb Specialists

Green Magic Herb Seeds
P. O. Box 8061
Ottawa, Ont.
K1G 3H6

Otto Richter & Sons Ltd.
Box 26
Goodwood, Ont.
L0C 1A0

Roses

Carl Pallek & Son
Box 137
Virgil, Ont.
L0S 1T0

Pickering Nurseries Inc.
670 Kingston Rd.
Pickering, Ont.
L1V 1A6

Springwood Miniature Roses
R. R. 3
Caledon East, Ont.
L0N 1E0

Mini Rose Nursery
P. O. Box 873
Guelph, Ont.
N1H 6M6

Landscaping
Walter Kuettel
86 Cambridge Cres.
Richmond Hill, Ont.
L4C 2G6

PRINCE EDWARD ISLAND

Vesey's Seeds Ltd.
Little York, P.E.I.
C0A 1P0

QUEBEC

Les Herbes Fines de Saint-
    Antoine
480 Chemin l'Acadie
St. Antoine-sur-Richelieu, Que.
J0L 1R0

J. Labonté & Fils
560 Chemin Chambly
Longueuil, Que.
J4H 3L8

Laval Seeds Inc.
3505 Boul. St. Martin Ouest
Ville de Laval, Que.
H7T 1A2

W. H. Perron
515 Boul. LaBelle
Ville de Laval, Que.
H7S 2A6

SASKATCHEWAN

Hardy Plant Nursery
P. O. Box 682
Airport Rd.
North Battleford, Sask.
S9A 2Y9

Honeywood Fruit and Bulb Farm
Box 63
Parkside, Sask.
S0J 2A0

Moon Lake Gardens Ltd.
1030 Ave. L South
Saskatoon, Sask.
S7M 2J5

Paper Birch Nurseries
Box 1
Paynton, Sask.
S0M 2J0

River Bend Nursery
P. O. Box 863
Estevan, Sask.
S4A 2A7

UNITED STATES

Gilbert H. Wild & Son, Inc.
(ship to Canada; peonies,
   iris, day lilies)
Sarcoxie, Missouri
U.S.A.
64862

SKOOT   If not in supply at
your local nursery, write to:

Plant Products Co. Ltd.
314 Orenda Rd.
Brampton, Ont.
L6T 1G1

Books

All About Roses. San Francisco: Ortho Books, 1983.

Bailey, Liberty H. *How Plants Get Their Names*. New York: Dover, 1933.
——. *Manual of Cultivated Plants*. Rev. ed. New York: Macmillan, 1949.

Bent, Arthur C. *Life Histories of North American Cardinals, Grosbeaks, Buntings, Tohees, Finches, Sparrows, and Their Allies*. 3 vols. New York: Dover, 1968.

——. *Life Histories of North American Flycatchers, Larks, Swallows and Their Allies*. New York: Dover, 1942.

Biles, Roy E. *The Complete Book of Garden Magic*. Chicago: J.G. Ferguson, 1951.

Bull, John, and John Farrand Jr. *The Audubon Society Field Guide to North American Birds*. New York: Alfred A. Knopf, 1977.

Clarkson, Rosetta E. *Herbs and Savory Seeds*. New York: Dover, 1972.

Findhorn Community. *Findhorn Garden*. New York: Harper and Row, 1976.

Hill, Lewis. *Pruning Simplified*. Pownal, Vt.: Garden Way, 1986.

Hosie, R. *Native Trees of Canada*. Don Mills, Ont.: Fitzhenry and Whiteside, 1979.

Garner, R.J. *The Grafter's Handbook*. London: Faber, 1979.

Harrison, Colin. *A Field Guide to the Nests, Eggs and Nestlings of North American Birds*. Toronto: Collins, 1984.

Leitch, Adelaide. *Into the High County*. The Corporation of the County of Dufferin, Ontario/Canada, 1975.

New Pronouncing Dictionary of Plant Names. Chicago: The Florists' Publishing Co., 1964.

Sackville-West, Victoria. *Victoria Sackville-West's Garden Book*. New York: Atheneum, 1983.

Slater, Paddy. *The Yellow Briar*. Toronto: Macmillan, 1970.

Time-Life Encyclopedia of Gardening, The. Rev. ed. New York: Time-Life Books, 1973.

Wilson, Helen Van Pelt. *Helen Van Pelt Wilson's Own Garden and Landscape Book*. Garden City, N.Y.: Doubleday, 1973.

——. *The New Perennials Preferred*. New York: Barrows, 1961.

Wynne, Peter. *Apples*. New York: Hawthorn, 1975.

Index